Traveling the Santa Fe Trail in the 21st Century

Driving Modern Roads Along Historic Santa Fe Trail

Written by Mary Allbeck
Photographs by Rebecca Strutz

With special quest editor
Lois Allbeck

Copyright © 2012 Mary Allbeck
All rights reserved.
ISBN-10: 1461191645
ISBN-13: 978-1461191643

Table of Contents

Forward 4
Dedication...7
Getting to the Starting Point..10
   A little history is in order. 11
Independence, Missouri...13
   Bingham-Waggoner Estate 20
   Other Places to See Nearby 22
Bonner Springs, Kansas...24
Olathe, Kansas 26
Gardner, Kansas..27
Lanesfield School House 29
Council Grove, Kansas...30
   Farmers & Drovers Bank..30
   Madonna of the Trail 33
   M-K-T Depot   (Missouri-Kansas-Texas).....................35
   Pioneer Cowboy Jail 36
   THE Council Oak (stump) 37
   Neosho River Crossing 39
   Terwilliger Home 41
Tallgrass Prairie Natl Preserve 42
   Spring Hill Farm and Stock Ranch 43
   Guided Tours 44
   Three Story Barn..45
   Cistern and Ice House..47
   Lower Fox Creek School 47
   Frontcountry Trails 48
   Backcountry Trails...48
Heading West, on US 56 50
Lyons, Kansas 54
Ellinwood, Kansas 56
Historical Markers on US 56 57
   Historical Marker – Cow Creek Station 57
   Cross Statue – Fray Juan de Padilla............................58
Ralph's Ruts 60
Fort Larned, Kansas 67
Santa Fe Trail Center 75
Garfield, Kansas..76

Dodge City, Kansas 77
Santa Fe Trail Tracks, US Survey Team 79
Cimarron, Kansas 81
Charlie's Ruts 84
Lakin, Kansas 87
Lamar, Colorado 92
Bent's Fort, Colorado 95
La Junta, Colorado 102
   La Junta Local Sights 103
On the Road – Highway 350 105
   Iron Spring Historic Area 106
   Pinon Canyon Maneuver Site 108
   High Desert Landscapes 111
Trinidad, Colorado 112
   A.R. Mitchell Museum & Gallery 119
   Trinidad History Museum 120
   Highway 25 heading South. 121
Raton Pass 122
   Other sights nearby - Capulin Volcano 126
Highway 25 into New Mexico 128
   Wagon Mound 129
Ft Union National Monument 130
   Fort Union Hospital Ruins 133
Highway 25 – Glorietta Pass 136
Santa Fe, New Mexico 137
   The La Fonda Hotel 140
Elevation Chart 145
Old Time Recipies 146
   Carne De Olla 146
   Chili Con Carne 147
   Jalapeno Cornbread 148
Montage of Terrain Changes 149
References 155
I N D E X 156

Forward

The purpose of this book is to guide modern day travelers along the historic Santa Fe Trail, using our modern day roads. Some places to eat, rest, and visit are listed, but it is beyond the scope of this book to try and duplicate travel books for Kansas City, MO, or Dodge City, KS. Rather, this book is a guide for modern day Trail travelers and somewhat of a memoir of the adventure of the Trail with my sister Becky Strutz, and our mother, Lois Allbeck.

My mother is a retired schoolteacher. When our family traveled the United States, we always had to stop at Historical Markers and check them out. (Dad called them Hysterical Markers.) So when Mom wanted to visit the modern day Santa Fe Trail, I knew I had to go along for the adventure.

View of **Fisher's Peak** (9,627) when leaving Trinidad, CO on the Santa Fe Trail, heading to Raton Pass.

We each started planning for the trip in our own way. Mom started looking for places to visit. I looked for a map that showed the historic Trail and modern day roads, but did not find any until we got to the actual states. There is a lot of information on the internet about the Trail and modern roads, but it is broken up by sections of the Trail, and I could not find a map of the Trail in its entirety.

When I travel I like to buy a travel book about the place I am visiting, but I could not find such a book for the modern day Santa Fe Trail. That's why I am writing this book. I did a MapQuest on the route and found that it would be about 800 miles. We spent 8 days on The Trail, but there is a lot to see, and you could take as much time as you like.

When I travel, I like to bring home food items like candy, salsa, spice mixes, and so forth. It's an edible souvenir that brings up memories of our adventure on the Santa Fe Trail.

Mom has a disabled placard, and it was very useful for parking closer to some of the places we stopped.

Bent's Old Fort, near La Junta, Colorado

Look for these symbols in the book:

- Disabled Parking Advantage
- Don't Miss!
- Fancy Food
- Food
- Gift Shop Alert!
- Lodging
- Sorry we missed it

Our destination - Santa Fe! This is the Santa Fe Plaza.

Dedication

We would like to dedicate this book to our parents, Alton and Lois Allbeck, who bravely traveled with their 6 children in a station wagon, in order to see the USA first hand. (Are we there yet?)

Our family traveled all over the USA, starting from Toledo, Ohio. When we moved to Riverside, CA we stopped to see the sights along the way.

Sarah, Mary, Betsy, Martha, Lois, Becky, and David

Martha remembers how Dad would take a green stick from a sapling and whittle one end to strip off the bark to expose the clean new wood. Then we would mold Bisquick mix on the end of the stick, and roast them over the campfire until they turned browned. The roasted treat slid off the stick and we would fill them with butter and jelly. YUM!!

My dad was very inventive, says Mary. He made a plywood box for the family to haul our camping gear on top of the car, since the station wagon was full of people. He painted 'The Allbecks' on the side of the box, and decorated it with stickers from all the places we visited.

Allbeck Family Crossing Arkansas River – summer 1963

As the eldest, Sarah got to enjoy many family trips. On one trip to Texas, Mom had used AAA to map the trip, but the maps were sketchy. One section of road had just about any kind of old pole to use as telephone poles and it looked funny. We came to a river with no bridge, Dad honked the horn and a ferry came and carried us across the river. I remember that we all sang like crazy to pass the time. Whoever did not behave had to sit between Mom and Dad.

Alton Allbeck, 1963

David tells of a trip to Vancouver, Canada to go camping on Vancouver Island. Our station wagon drove onto a huge ferry for the trip over to the island. We were right next to a lake and we made a raft from tree branches we

8

collected and we rafted around for a while. The raft mostly sank.

Becky made a list of memories:
1. I loved the way Dad would always sing in the car.
2. Also, Dad would always tell the best campfire stories. I loved his homemade hotdog & marshmallow sticks. Remember he made them out of a coat hanger and they had a wood handle?
3. I have always been amazed how Mom did this. She kept the little makeshift kitchen up and running for days on end. It was fun to wash dishes outside and to eat at the picnic tables.
4. We each had a 'Charlie Chip' box that we painted for our cloths. They packed and stacked easily.

Martha, Lois, David, Betsy, Mary, Alton

Betsy remembers a family trip to Washington DC was the first trip we took as a family with the tent. Becky was still in the stroller, so it must have been in the early 1960s. We drove from Toledo, Ohio to Washington DC in our station wagon. I remember that we usually stayed at KOA campgrounds. Mom thought they were clean and safe. We stayed at a KOA that was close to Washington DC so we could go into the city every day. I believe the first thing we went to see was the Washington Monument. Dad had luck with parking. As busy as Washington DC is, Dad found a place to park right in front.

Getting to the Starting Point

This adventure starts in Kansas City, MO, and ends in Albuquerque, NM.

If you need to fly to get to the Santa Fe Trail Starting point, then book a flight to the
Kansas City, Missouri Airport, http://www.flykci.com/

At the end of the trip, return the rental car at the airport in Albuquerque, NM and fly home. Book your return home flight leaving from **Albuquerque New Mexico** http://www.cabq.gov/airport

Free maps and Travel Guides are available in all three states at Visitor Information Centers and hotel lobbies.

Rent a big, comfortable vehicle that can hold all the passengers, their luggage, and items purchased during the trip. We drove this Chrysler 300 with three people, and by the end of the trip the rear passenger seat was filled up with our 'treasures'.

Our 'Sweet Ride', parked at the start of the adventure in Independence, MO near the Jackson County Courthouse

A little history is in order.

In a nutshell, the Spanish in Santa Fe did not welcome traders from the United States. They wanted to keep all of the trade business with Santa Fe within the family, since Mexico was one of their colonies. When the Mexicans eventually won their independence from Spain, the American traders were welcomed with open arms.

In 1807, Lt. Zebulon M. Pike and his party were captured, taken to Santa Fe, and imprisoned in Chihuahua for venturing into Spanish territory. They were later released the same year at the border of Louisiana.

SF Trail Factoid #1
The Santa Fe Trail was successfully opened as a commercial route in 1821. It was in use only 59 years, from 1821 to 1880. The trail head kept moving westward as the Santa Fe Railroad was built and new sections of rail were completed.

In 1810, the Mexican push for independence from Spain started with an uprising by Father Hidalgo on Sept. 16, 1810, unfortunately, he lost the battle and was captured and executed. The struggle was to continue for 10 more years. Thinking that it would be safe to go to Santa Fe, in 1812 James Baird lead an expedition of twelve men to Santa Fe where they were arrested by the authorities and imprisoned in Chihuahua for twelve years, basically for trespassing.

In 1815, two fur traders were given permission by the Spanish governor to trap and trade in the northern mountains, which they did for two years, until a new governor rescinded their privileges. They were arrested, imprisoned in Santa Fe, court-martialed, and kicked out of the dominions of Spain.

The Santa Fe Trail opened in 1821, when William Becknell left Franklin, MO with a small trading party looking to trade with Indians. Not finding any Indians, they traveled on a in a southwesterly direction into Spanish territory. Near the upper Canadian river, they were surprised by Mexican dragoons and expected to be arrested. But the political situation had changed, and they were welcomed by the Mexicans, who escorted them to Santa Fe. Becknell and his party made a profit of 1,500% from their trade goods, which encouraged them to come back the next year. Becknell is credited as being the Father of the Santa Fe Trail because he found a good mode of transportation in the wagons and the passable wagon route.

The Santa Fe Trail closed in 1880, when the railroad reached Santa Fe. No need for the wagons hauled by oxen or mules anymore.

Our modern highways follow the route of the Old Trail in many places. Starting in Olathe, KS, take Highway 56 west, to Kinsley, KS, where Highway 56 and Highway 50 merge. Continue westward, and turn south on Highway 350 near La Junta, CO. Continue south on 350 to Trinidad, CO, and then take Interstate 25 to Santa Fe, NM.

SF Trail Factoid #70
The Arkansas River is a major tributary of the Mississippi River. The Arkansas generally flows to the east and southeast as it traverses the U.S. states of Colorado, Kansas, Oklahoma, and Arkansas.

The Santa Fe Trail follows the Arkansas River westward through Kansas and Colorado, and turns south at the Purgatory River, thus avoiding the continental divide. The Trail then crosses Raton Pass into the high desert plains of New Mexico.

12

Independence, Missouri

Jackson County Courthouse
201 W Lexington Ave
Independence, MO 64050

We started our journey retracing the steps of the Santa Fe Trail, in front of the Jackson County Courthouse in Independence, Missouri. It's a beautiful brick building, built in 1836, that replaced the first structure built in 1828. Wagons would gather here in order to join a wagon train to Santa Fe.

Jackson County Courthouse

SF Trail Factoid #1

The Santa Fe Trail was successfully opened as a commercial route in 1821. It was in use only 59 years, from 1821 to 1880. The trail head kept moving westward as the Santa Fe Railroad was built and new sections of rail were completed.

Take your time and walk around the area near the square. There are a lot of small shops, and restaurants.

Just Taffy 204 N Liberty St, Independence, Missouri. This store makes all its own fudge, and 14 kinds of taffy. Stock up on sweets for the road trip.

Luscious tasting Montana Wild Blueberry Jam is made for Just Taffy, according to the label. It has juicy whole blueberries because it is a jam, not a jelly.

Rheinland Restaurant
http://www.rheinlandrestaurant.com/
208 North Main Street,
Independence, Missouri
We ate here because we thought we would not see too many German restaurants on the Trail. We were right.

> SF Trail Factoid #4
> The original starting point of the Trail was in Franklin, Missouri, but it was badly damaged by floods in 1828. Travelers avoided 100 miles of troublesome roads by embarking from Independence instead.

The Uptown Boutique, located at the corner of N. Liberty and W. Maple, is adjacent to the Courthouse square.

Gilbert, Whitney & Co.

104 North Liberty
Independence, Missouri, 64050

Open 10am-6pm, Monday-Saturday - 816.836.0578
http://gilbertwhitney.net

Housed in a building that dates back to 1832, this former J.C. Penny's store is now home to Gilbert, Whitney & Co. Once a mercantile store for those heading west, it now sells gourmet groceries & kitchenware.

SF Trail Factoid #71
At 1,469 miles (2,364 km), the Arkansas River is the sixth longest river in the United States, the second-longest tributary in the Mississippi-Missouri system, and the 45th longest river in the world.

Clinton's Soda Fountain
100 W. Maple, Independence, Missouri
Hours: Monday – Saturday 11am – 8pm, closed Sundays
http://www.clintonssodafountain.com/

Clinton's Soda Fountain sells old fashioned ice cream, shakes, and phosphates, plus pastries and coffee. Harry Truman worked his first job here.

SF Trail Factoid #3
Early in the 1900s the route of the Santa Fe Trail was marked by the DAR (Daughters of the American Revolution), who placed 175 of the stone markers. About 100 of the markers are in Kansas.

16

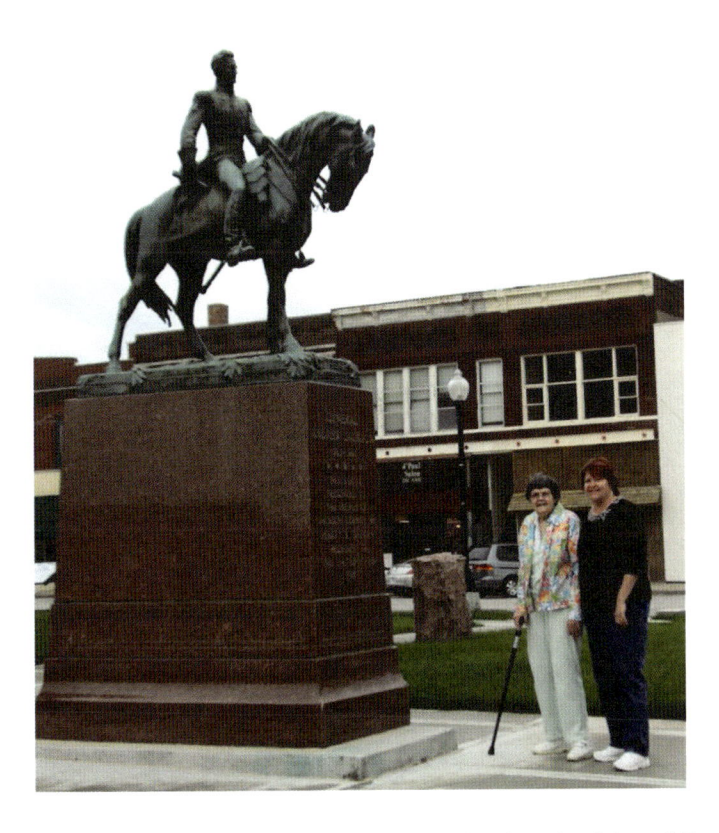

Statue of General Jackson on the back side of the Jackson County Courthouse, with Lois and Mary.

SF Trail Factoid #74
Many nations of Native Americans lived near, or along, the 1,450 mile (2334 km) stretch of the Arkansas River for thousands of years. The first Europeans to see the river were members of the Spanish Coronado expedition on June 29, 1541. Also in the 1540s, Hernando de Soto discovered the junction of the Arkansas with the Mississippi. The name "Arkansas" was first applied by Father Jacques Marquette, who called the river *Akansa* in his journal of 1673.

National Trails Museum

318 W. Pacific, Independence, MO 64050.
Telephone: (816) 325-7575.

Open	9 a.m. to 4:30 p.m. Monday through Saturday
	12:30 - 4:30 p.m. Sunday.

Admission – Adults $6, Seniors (62+) $5
	Youth (6 – 17) $3, under 6 free

Don't miss the award winning film **'West'**. This 17 minute film gives an overview of America's westward expansion, and helps give you an appreciation of what you are seeing in the National Trails Museum exhibits.

http://www.ci.independence.mo.us/nftm/Default.aspx

Postcards from the Gift Shop:

Archetypical Prospector with his faithful donkey toting all of his necessities.

Wagons leaving Bent's Fort

Independence, Missouri in the early days.

18

This is a photo of a Conestoga wagon at the National Trails Museum. This particular wagon is a replica made by a man in Kansas then donated to the museum. He modeled it after an original wagon in the Kansas State Historical Society in Topeka, Kansas. It's in the room where the movie is shown.

This really big map shows the three trails – Santa Fe, Oregon, and California - as they start in Independence and go their separate ways.

19

Gift Shop Alert!

Very nice gift shop, with a selection of items made in the USA.

You won't see a gift shop as nice as this one for a long, long time.

Here is a list of some of the items sold at the National Trails Museum Gift Shop:

- Beginning Quilting Kit
- Beth's Market Basket Kit
- Children's Pioneer Bonnet
- Craft kits
- Hurdy Gurdy
- Harmonica Necklace
- NFTM Collector Spoon
- Pioneer Stew mix
- Artwork
- Books
- DVDs
- Postcards
- Handmade trivets

Bingham-Waggoner Estate

313 West Pacific Ave, Independence, Missouri

Right across street from the National Trails Museum, the first of many ruts and/or swales to come.

This painting, 'Trails Leaving Independence – 1837', from the National Trails Museum, shows wagons leaving Independence, Missouri. Wagons traveling in an unorganized manner across the open land left wagon ruts just like the ones seen at the Bingham-Waggoner Estate where they rudely cut through the Estate, damaging the farm land as they go.

Wagons went charging over this pasture on the Bingham-Waggoner Estate on their way to Santa Fe.

21

Other Places to See Nearby

Community of Christ International Headquarters

From downtown Independence, the distinctive spire of the Community of Christ International Headquarters can be seen. It is located at the corner of River and Walnut,.

Guided tours
Mon – Sat   9am to 4pm
Sun – 1pm to 4pm

www.CofChrist.org

Harry S. Truman Library and Museum

500 W. US Hwy. 24,
Independence MO 64050
Phone: 816-268-8200 or 1-800-833-1225;

truman.library@nara.gov;

Very interesting and informative museum of Missouri's favorite native son. He was president for 8 years, and guided the United States through the ending of World War II, dropping the atom bomb, formation of the United Nations, and the successful operation of the Berlin Airlift.

Lois and the American Flag outside of the Harry S. Truman Library and Museum.

Bonner Springs, Kansas

Back N Thyme –
Guest House and Herb Garden

1100 South 130th Street
Bonner Springs KS 66012
(913) 422-5207
http://www.backnthyme.com/

Absolutely beautiful, peaceful, and comfortable, this bed and breakfast is a wonderful way to start your journey down the Santa Fe Trail. All the rooms are unique and tastefully decorated with a theme – The Sweet Annie Room, the Rosemary Room, and the Bay Laurel Room. Take a look at their website for descriptions of the rooms.

Wine and nibbles were served at 6pm on the day we arrived. Breakfast was served at 9am and included coffee, selection of teas, mufins, fresh fruit, quiche, and fresh ornge juice.

Back N Thyme is nestled into the countryside, surrounded by trees, and is typical of what the natural scenery is like in the Independence, MO area.

Beautiful tranquil setting typical of eastern Kansas woodlands.

View of the pond and sitting area at Back N Thyme in Bonner Springs, Kansas.

The three travelers pose for a photo before leaving the comfort of Back N Thyme and heading down the Trail on Highway 56.

SF Trail Factoid #44

The Mahaffie Farmstead and Stagecoach Stop, near Olathe, KS, was used as a stagecoach stop from 1865 – 1869 for three different stage lines. It is the only known Santa Fe Trail station that is open to the public. Owned and operated by the city of Olathe.

Olathe, Kansas

We started off on our journey down the Santa Fe Trail at the town of Olathe, KS, where we got off Interstate 35. That was the last we saw of multiple highway lanes each direction. We were on highway 56 and 50 for the rest of Kansas; a beautiful drive across the heartland of America.

Right where you get off the freeway is the Mahaffie Stagecoach Stop and Farm.

1200 Kansas City Road in Olathe, Kansas

Tours are available:
Wed – Sat. 10am - 4pm
Sun. 12 noon – 4pm
$3.25 adults, $2.00 children 5 - 12.
Closed Mondays and Tuesdays

You can wander around the farm and pet the horses and livestock for free. There is an old Ice House, where big chunks of ice were stored back before there was any refrigeration. Chunks of ice from a nearby lake were cut and hauled to the ice house, or snow was compacted inside the house and saved for the summer months. Check out the nice litle museum, in a building that is a reconstruction of the original farm. Lots of artifacts from the farm's long history.

Driving Directions – Once you turn off the main highway onto US 56 at Olathe, KS, say goodbye to the big city, and hello to green fields for the rest of the drive through Kansas.

Our journey then continues down highway 56, heading west. The countryside here is very flat and emerald green. There is a feeling of being in the middle of a wide open expanse, a feeling of being free and connected to nature.

Gardner, Kansas

Highway 56 passes through downtown Gardner, KS, where the roadway changes to bricks, which are very striking. Bricks seem to be the most common building material in the area. Farther on down the Trail, stone was used more often than brick. People built with the natural resources available to them.

Continue driving down highway 56, west of Gardner, KS, heading for Council Grove, KS. At this point, Highway 56 closely follows the historic Santa Fe Trail heading in a westerly direction, following the natural flow of the land.

Historic brick schoolhouse still seems to be in use, judging by the swing sets.

Highway 56 and Road U. Nothing but peace and tranquility, unless you brought children who would be saying 'are we there yet?'

SF Trail Factoid #13

Missouri Mules are really from Mexico. The first "Missouri Mules' were brought to Missouri from Santa Fe in 1823 by 'Major' Stephen Cooper, an American trader. The oxen were very tired and needed rest, so fresh mules were bought for the return trip, who then found a new home in Missouri.

Lanesfield School House

18745 S. Dillie Rd, Edgerton, KS 66021, Price: free
Hours: open 1-5pm, Tuesday – Sunday

Lanesfield School House, which is a Kansas Historic Site. It's near the intersection of W. 157th Street and Dillie Road, 3 miles southwest of Gardner, KS.

Built in 1869, it's the last original building left of the town of Lanesfield, Kansas. The school teacher taught grades 1 to 8 in the subjects of geography, reading, spelling, arithmetic, and penmanship. It's all set up as it used to be for the children to come to school. Inside the door is a cloakroom, and then around the corner into the schoolroom are the desks and chalkboards.

Prairie surrounds the Lanesfield School House.

Imagine what it would have been like to be a student there.

Council Grove, Kansas

On Highway 56, heading west from Olathe, Kansas.

This is a delightful town to visit. Many historical sites are in town, and a short drive to Tallgrass Prairie National Preserve.

The first of the 'Madonna of the Trail' statues that you will see is just past this marker.

Farmers & Drovers Bank

Built in 1892, this two-story red brick building with stone trim is a well-preserved example of eclectic architecture with brick and stone masonry, Romanesque arches, a Byzantine dome and minarets. The bank reflects the growing sophistication and prosperity of the area before the turn of the 20th century, yet today operates in a current state-of-the-art environment. It is located at the corner of Neosho and Main Street.

SF Trail Factoid #37

Some Santa Fe traders opened a trading post at Council Grove in 1847, placing Seth Hayes in charge.

🛏 The Cottage House Hotel

25 North Neosho, Council Grove, Kansas 66846
620-767-6828   1-800-727-7903,
www.cottagehousehotel.com

Located just off Highway 56, a block from Main Street, this rambling two-story brick building began in 1867 as a three-room cottage and blacksmith shop. The Cottage House Hotel continued to grow in stages, including construction in 1871, 1898, and 1913.

From Aunt Minnie's Room to the Anniversary Suite, every room in the small hotel has a personality all its own. Special accents in each room might range from stained glass windows to a clawfoot bathtub. Selected antique furnishings and lace curtains are featured throughout the building. All the rooms at the Cottage House Hotel offer a unique combination of period furnishing and modern comforts. There is a self-serve restaurant and gift shop on the first floor.

A tornado warning sign is posted in the hotel hallway, just in case you forgot you were in Kansas.

Gift Shop Alert! Aunt Jo's Gift Parlor,
in the lobby of the Cottage House

Very nice gift shop that sells collectables such as dolls, soap, spoons, coffee mugs, Kansas postcards, T-shirts, souvenirs, gifts, and Victorian collectibles.

Hays House Tavern and Restaurant
112 W Main St, Council Grove, KS,
(620) 767-5611
Open Monday through Sunday, but closed Sunday evenings.

In 1857, Seth M. Hays opened the Hays House Tavern and Restaurant, making it the oldest continuously operating restaurant west of the Mississippi River. Its customers have included Jesse James and George Armstrong Custer.

SF Trail Factoid #57
Seth Hays was the first permanent white settler in Council Grove. He was a great grandson of Daniel Boone, and a cousin of Kit Carson.

Hays House serves country food with generous servings. House specialties include skillet fried chicken, crunch chicken salad, Beulah's Ham, prime rib, and great pies.

32

Madonna of the Trail

Erected in Council Grove in 1928 by the Daughters of the American Revolution, the Madonna of the Trail depicts a pioneer mother with her two children. These pink Algonite stone statues were placed in communities on the National Old Trails Road in 12 states.

There is another one in Lamar, CO, next to the train station and visitor center.

The twelve Madonna monuments are in different states of the Union in these locations:
- Bethesda, Maryland
- Washington County, Pennsylvania
- Wheeling, West Virginia
- Springfield, Ohio
- Vandalia, Illinois
- Lexington, Missouri
- Richmond, Indiana
- Council Grove, Kansas
- Lamar, Colorado
- Albuquerque, New Mexico
- Springerville, Arizona
- Upland, California

The Madonna of the Trail is a pioneer woman clasping her baby with her young son clinging to her skirts. The statues are made of Algonite stone with the main aggregate being pink Missouri granite. The statues stand 10 feet high on top of a six foot base with a five foot foundation.

The statues honor the pioneer mothers who travelled west along trails like the Santa Fe.

SF Trail Factoid #66
J.H. Foster passed through Council Grove in the year 1849, with a caravan of freighters. He said there was only one house on the Trail, about 110 miles from the start of the journey. At this time, there were only a few log cabins west of the Neosho crossing.

Marker commemorating Company C, 137th Infantry, Santa Fe Trail Division

M-K-T Depot   (Missouri-Kansas-Texas)

On Main Street in Council Grove there a many historical sites.

One of only two M-K-T depots remaining on their original sites in Kansas. The original depot was built in 1869, but destroyed by fire in 1894.

www.katydepot.com

A new depot was built later that year. The line was abandoned in 1957, and the railroad station building currently serves as a shop for antiques and unique collectibles called the Katy Depot, located at 512 E. Main Street.

The shop selling soap, candles, honey, art and woodwork items, as well as antiques, is open Wednesday thru Sunday. (620) 767-8294

SF Trail Factoid #65

There was no post office west of council Grove and the next stop for the Overland mail was Fort Union or Bent's Fort a trading station located 650 miles or seventeen days from Independence, MO. After this the next stop for the mail was Santa Fe.

35

Pioneer Cowboy Jail
City Calaboose since 1849

"Only jail in early days on the old Santa Fe Trail. Within its walls desperadoes, border ruffians and robbers were held. During the Indian raid of 1859, two Indians were taken out and hanged by a mob. A bad man, Jack McDowell, was hanged from the Neosho River bridge after being guarded in the building. Jack the Peeper was shot while trying to escape, after terrifying the town for months. This building has housed many bootleggers since 1880. Also some who ran stills producing moonshine whiskey……"   "G. Bill" Coffin in his: The Story of the Old Jail

This jail is in tiny inside! There are two cells that look like they could hold one man each, and not comfortably. Imagine if the whole gang was arrested and shoved into this jail.

DAR Marker – 1906

SF Trail Factoid #63

This was the only jail on the Santa Fe Trail between Westport (Kansas City) and the foreign city of Santa Fe, New Mexico, a route of 780 miles.

36

THE Council Oak (stump)

E. Main Street (US 56) near N. 4th Street

The original tree is now a stump that is protected from the elements by a roof built over it.

A council meeting was held under this tree August 10, 1825, attended by three U.S. Commissioners and the Osage Indians. The resulting treaty gave Americans and Mexicans free passage along the Santa Fe Trail through Osage Territory in return for $800. It was also at this time that Council Grove got its name. The Council Oak was part of a mile wide grove of trees that provided shelter and wood for wagon repair on the Santa Fe Trail. Before it blew down during a windstorm in 1958, the oak was approximately 70 feet high and measured 16 feet around.

Lois and Mary do their best 'Vanna White' impersonations at the site of the Council Grove stump.

37

The original Council Oak probably looked a lot like this tree in the Neosho River Crossing Park.

The authors take a break for lunch in Council Grove at The Station.

Note the painting of travelers on the Santa Fe Trail behind Lois.

The Station
219 W Main St, Council Grove, KS
(620) 767-5619

Neosho River Crossing

One of the most documented river crossings of the Santa Fe Trail, the natural rockbed crossing over the Neosho River can best be seen from the north side of the Neosho River Bridge on Main Street.

This picture shows the historic bridge foundation next to the modern day bridge and gas station. The easy slope of the land into the river combined with a solid rock riverbed that is safer to cross make it the best place for wagons to cross the Neosho River.

Last Chance Store

Erected by Tom Hill in 1857, the Last Chance Store was, for a brief period of time, the last chance for freighters bound for Santa Fe to pick up supplies for their journey, hence it's name. It is also the oldest commercial building in Council Grove. The building served as post office facilities, government trading house, and polling place.

SF Trail Factoid #67

Council Grove is perhaps the only city in America to have the present Main Street on the exact route of the original Santa Fe Trail. The famous Hays Hotel and Café (1857) are original buildings used on the Trail. The Rumsey White hardware store building (1850) was used by Santa Fe Trail traffic.

Terwilliger Home

The Terwilliger Home was built in 1861, and is one of four oldest homes remaining alongside the Santa Fe Trail. It was the last house in Council Grove that Santa Fe freighters passed as they proceeded west, and was a welcome sight on their return trip, as it signaled their return to civilization.

This restored home houses the **Trail Days Bakery Café**, known for excellent food served in a historic atmosphere.
803 West Main Street, Council Grove, Kansas 66846
Open Mon – Sat. 11am to 8pm   (620) 767-7986

http://kansastravel.org/traildaysbakery.htm

Also see at this site in Council Grove an authentic log house, a one-room schoolhouse and unique tourist camp cabins.

Tallgrass Prairie Natl Preserve

Don't Miss!
16 miles south of Council Grove on Highway 117

Hours:
The historic ranch headquarters is open 9am to 4:30pm daily (except Thanksgiving, Christmas, and new Year's Day)

Admission:
No admission charge, and most activities are free.

Disabled Parking Advantage
Disabled parking is up the hill to the back of the barn.

Don't miss the excellent film about history of Tallgrass shown in the Barn, and the museum showing Kansas farm life.

Spring Hill Farm and Stock Ranch

Cattleman Stephan F. Jones founded the Spring Hill Farm and Stock Ranch, and built his home in 1881 with hand-cut limestone. The 11 room house is characteristic of the Second Empire style of 19th century architecture. The water springs on the hillside provide water to the house – thus the name, Spring Hill Farm and Stock Ranch. Nearby is the massive three-story limestone barn, ice house, and garden.

Gift Shop Alert!
The bookstore/gift shop in the ranch house is open daily.

Visitors may purchase books for children and adults, prints, postcards, educational and hand-crafter gift items, natural objects, and items related to local culture.

Guided Tours

House Tours are conducted through the historic 1881 limestone ranch house May through October.

Bus Tours of the Prairie
11am, 1pm and 3pm
$5 per adult, $3 age 5 – 18, 4 and under free
Advance reservations are recommended, but arrangements can be made the day of your visit if space is available. Call 620-273-8494.

See the diversity of the Tallgrass Prairie National Reserve on this 6.4 mile bus tour lead by National Park Service rangers. While touring the preserve's backcountry, you will learn about the Indians, the geology that formed the Flint Hills, and the legacy of ranching. Experience the vast prairie landscape – sweeping views, rolling hills, and an endless sky. The tour lasts about 90 minutes and is available daily from the last Saturday in April through the last Sunday in October.

Three Story Barn

The massive 60 x 110 foot barn was used to house animals, shelter equipment from the elements, and store the hay and grain that fed the livestock during the winter months. In 1885, Jones's livestock numbered 20 swine, 30 horses, 8 milk cows, 4 mules, and hundreds of cattle foraging on the ranch's prairie grasses. The barn was built into the side of the hill for natural insulation and access.

Rear view of the 2nd and 3rd levels of the barn.

Described in 1883 as 'the best improved farm in Chase county', the Spring Hill Farm and Stock Ranch became a showpiece for cattleman Stephen F. Jones and his wife Louisa. In 1878 they came to Kansas from Colorado wishing to graze cattle on the 'fine prairie grasses' of the Flint Hills and then ship them by rail to market in Kansas City. His ranch grew to 7,000 acres, specializing in Hereford, Durham, and Galloway cattle. During the 1880s, ranching was moving from open range to enclosed pasture grazing.

Animals lived on the barn's first level, where there are stalls and pens for them. The animals could walk out the barn door directly into the pasture.

The second level of the barn was used to store harnesses, and various farm items and equipment.

Harness collars for teams of horses are shown here.

They slip over the horse's head onto the shoulder, and enable the horse to pull the wagon or plow.

46

Cistern and Ice House

A cistern was built into the hillside to collect and store the cool spring water.

The cool water was piped underground and down the hill to the house.

Ice was preserved for use during the hot prairie summers by packing the ice in prairie hay or sawdust.

Lower Fox Creek School

Built in 1882, this one-room school provided a setting for educating local area students until 1930, when it was abandoned and reverted to the ranch owner.

Frontcountry Trails

The preserve's frontcountry nature trails are open year-round during daylight hours only. For visitor safety and resource preservation, you are asked to stay on designated trails.

The Southwind Nature Trail – a 1 ¾ mile hiking trail through the Tallgrass prairie, passing by the Lower Fox Creek School. Scenic overlook area offers a wide-open view of the prairie.

The Bottomland Trail – a ¾ mile loop or a shorter ½ mile loop through bottomland prairie along Fox Creek. Wayside exhibits and an information kiosk tell the story of the prairie restoration and cultural history in the area. This trail is wheelchair accessible and offers a comfort station.

Backcountry Trails

The preserve's backcountry day hiking trails are daily between 9am and 3:30pm from May through October and on weekends from November through April. Permits are required for the backcountry hiking trails. A limited number of permits will be issued daily and may be reserved in advance by calling the preserve at 620-273-8494.
- **Scenic Overlook Trail - 6.4 miles**
- **3 Pasture Loop Trail – 3.8 miles**
- **Red House Trail - 6 miles.**

Tallgrass Prairie National Preserve is an opportunity to experience the natural wonder and rich cultural history of the Kansas Flint Hills. The expansive rolling hills and wide-open vista of this Great Plains region are a rare remnant of the expanse of Tallgrass prairie that once covered 140 million acres of North America.

Once the hunting grounds of the Kansa and Osage Indians, the preserve's 10,894 acres are home to an astonishing variety of life: over 450 species of plants, 150 kinds of birds, 39 types of reptiles and amphibians, and 31 species of mammals. A cycle of climate, fire, and animal grazing – once buffalo, now cattle – has sustained this ecosystem.

Heading West, on US 56

When ready to leave Council Grove and head down the Trail, continue driving west on Highway US 56.

Back on the Trail after a restful night and breakfast at the Cottage Inn, we spied this collection of road signs, showing us the way forward on Highway US 56.

The road turns south in the town of Herington, KS, and then West again near Marion, KS.

SF Trail Factoid #16
Hudson Bay blankets were so valued by Indians and Hispanics that they were marked in points to indicate its value in beaver pelts.

50

Red farm buildings are seen nestled in the pastures and deep blue skies on a beautiful spring day.

> **SF Trail Factoid #54**
>
> Horses, mules, and oxen were used to haul wagons on the Trail. The most popular were oxen, and least popular were horses.

In Herington, KS on Highway US 56 the road turns south for few miles.

Highway US 56 turns west again near Marion, KS, and merges with Highway US 150 for a while.

Just stay on the main road and follow the signs for 56.

Mary poses next to stone marker showing the Chisholm Trail crossing the Santa Fe Trail just outside Canton, KS.

Livestock munching hay in a pen just off the highway.

Kansas has a lot of oil derricks. We saw many of these railroad tanker cars before we took a picture. It may not be historical Santa Fe Trail, but it's a big part of modern Kansas.

SF Trail Factoid #18
The teamster's diet while on the Trail consisted of flour, salt pork, coffee, and fresh meat killed along the way.

SF Trail Factoid #17
The major items taken on the return trip from New Mexico to Missouri were gold, silver, spices, silver bullion, gold dust, mules, donkeys, furs, buffalo robes, and wool.

Lyons, Kansas

http://skyways.lib.ks.us/towns/Lyonsm/

Coronado Quivira Museum
105 West Lyon
Lyons, KS
(620) 257-3941

Open Tuesday thru Saturday – 9 am to 5 pm
Closed Sunday and Monday, and major holidays.
Admission: $2 adults, $1 child 6 to 12, under 6 free

To get there from Highway US 56, turn South on East Ave S. It's located on the corner of East Ave S and West Lyon St.

Known as one of the best small museums in Kansas, its exhibits focus on the Santa Fe Trail, early inhabitants of the area, Spanish explorers, and the history of American settlement.

Statue of Mother and Child reading. This is right off Highway US 56 as you pass thru Lyons, KS.

SF Trail Factoid #58

Mail wagons were pulled by 4 mules, and carried enough corn to feed the mules for the entire trip to Santa Fe. Two extra mules were brought along as spares. The men would sleep under the wagon until enough corn had been consumed to make space for them in the wagon, under the canvas.

Ellinwood, Kansas

http://www.ellinwoodchamber.com/

Sorry we missed it -Underground Ellinwood

This town used to have an active underground section. Rapid growth in the 1870's and 1880's filled the business blocks of Ellinwood, KS from upstairs down to the basements. The lower level had a variety of store fronts and shops: drummer rooms, sample rooms, bath house, saloons, and meat storage. Typically shops changed locations from time to time. Ellinwood boasted of attorneys, hotels, a jewelry store, grain dealers, blacksmiths, boot makers, millenary shops, a brewery, dentists, general stores, billiard halls, lumber dealers, a newspaper along with a jail and a town band.

Hours: Tours Are Conducted Only by Advance Reservations - Very Welcomed! Tours Available daily - Adults $5.00
Physical Address: N.W. corner of Main & Santa Fe, U.S. 56 at the stoplight
Mailing Address: One North Main, PO Box 306
	Ellinwood, Kansas 67526-0306
Phone: 620-564-2400 – Bill Starr, Owner

John Henry Restaurant

518 E. Santa Fe Blvd (US 56), Ellinwood, KS
We came thru Ellinwood on a Sunday looking for lunch, and just about everything was closed. A local shopkeeper suggested we try John Henry, an unassuming portable building we had breezed by on our way in. I had the best hamburger – ever! That Kansas beef is really tasty.

Historical Markers on US 56

Historical Marker – Cow Creek Station

The sign says: 'One mile south is the hand-dug well that served the U.S. Cavalry and Santa Fe Trail travelers in the 1860s.

For five days in July, 1864, 600 Indians besieged a trading post near the well and a wagon train nearby. When the attackers tried to overrun the post, "Buffalo Bill" Mathewson fired a small cannon into the midst of several on horseback and afoot, ending the siege.

A later "Buffalo Bill", William F. Cody, worked at the site briefly before moving in 1867 to Ellsworth, where he gained the nickname by killing buffalo for railroad workers.

Cross Statue – Fray Juan de Padilla

On Highway US 50 between Lyons and Chase

The sign says: This Cross is erected to the memory of Father Padilla, Franciscan Missionary, who stood with Coronado at the erection of the first Christian Cross on these prairies. Father Padilla devoted his life to the service of the Cross and to the Indians of Quivira and suffered a martyr's death in that service in the year of our Lord 1542.

The symbol on the Cross is inscribed, Jesus Christ, Victor, and expresses the victory of faith and sacrifice. The square, quartered by the cross denotes the four corners of the world brought into Christian unity when Father Padilla carried the Cross of Christianity to the center of the new world. This monument is a gift to the People of Kansas by the Knights of Columbus of this State. Erected 1950.

Santa Fe Trail
1822 – 1872
Marked by the
Daughters of the American Revolution
and the
STATE OF KANSAS
1906

Lois and Becky admire a Santa Fe Trail Marker.

SF Trail Factoid #40

The first stagecoach and mail service over the Santa Fe Trail was established in 1850 by the Waldo, Hall and Company. The stage line started in Independence, MO and went to Santa Fe, NM. Fare was $125 in the summer and $150 in the winter. Stages departed monthly, and the baggage allowance was 40 pounds.

SF Trail Factoid #45

William 'Buffalo Bill' Mathewson operated a trading ranch near where the Trail crossed Cow Creek in Kansas. The well on his property is still preserved.

Ralph's Ruts

4 miles west of Chase on US 56. Turn Right on 4th Road from Highway US 56.

422 Ave L
Chase, Kansas 67527
(620) 938-2504

The address above is for the farmhouse; the ruts are located on 4th Road, just before it intersects with Ave L. We almost gave up on finding it, but turned the corner, and there it is!

How to spot a wagon rut from the Santa Fe Trail era:

Looking east, look for a series of swales in the natural prairie.

Look for a difference in the color and texture of the grass in the ruts. (I'm still not sure what this means.)

Look for lumpy spots. (Yeah, like, everywhere.) Look for sets of ruts running side by side, as the wagons traveled side by side and not in single file – and good luck!

Welcome to Ralphs Ruts, the first of many such stops to come.

Hey look! The Original Santa Fe Trail crossed the pasture right here!

Lois contemplates the natural beauty of Kansas, and the difficulty of spotting wagon ruts after 100 years.

Pawnee Rock

On Highway US 50 west of Great Bend, Kansas, turn right on SW 110th Ave, and follow the signs to the park.

The name Pawnee Rock refers to a town, as well as the actual sandstone bluff landmark.

http://www.legendsofkansas.com/pawneerock.html

Over the years, the natural stone outcropping was pillaged for building materials, and the original Pawnee Rock was decimated. In later years, the town of Pawnee Rock rebuilt the site up to the height of the original rock.

That's Mary standing on the upper level. There is a circular staircase in the corner brick support.

The local town of Pawnee Rock, KS, holds events at this park, which has a nice lawn and trees. Picnic tables are scattered about the park, which makes it an ideal place to stop and pull out the cooler.

Pawnee Rock was originally over 150 feet tall, but railroad construction removed 15 to 20 feet of the rock outcropping in the 18970s and used it for road bed material. Settlers who founded the town of Pawnee Rock also used the rock for building material for their town.

The sign says 'PLEASE DO NOT DEFACE THE ROCK'. This sign should have been up in the 1870s.

This prominent landmark is the halfway point on the Trail. It was important to all the people on the prairie. The Plains tribes used it as a lookout point to spy buffalo herds and wagon trails. Travelers on the trail welcomed the sight of Pawnee Rock, but also viewed it as a dangerous place where they might get ambushed. Hundreds of Trail travelers etched their names in the soft sandstone of Pawnee Rock.

Each side of the pillar has a different animal head.

This side shows a Buffalo head.

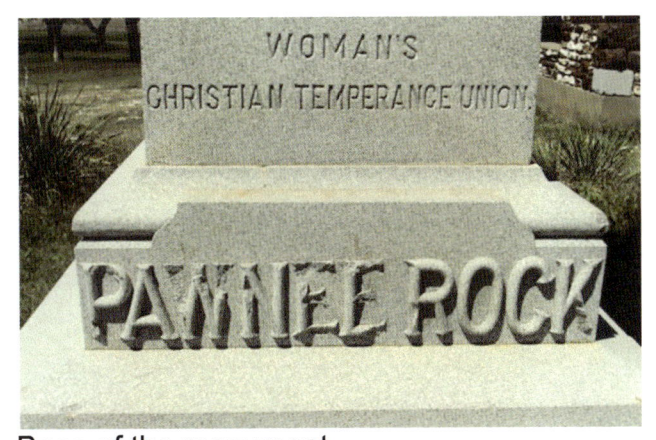

Base of the monument.

The stone monument at Pawnee Rock State Historic Site was dedicated on May 24, 1912 before a crowd of 8,000 onlookers.

65

Pawnee Rock; originally, the rock was 15 to 20 feet higher.

Close up of Pawnee Rock showing the sandstone rock layers.

Fort Larned, Kansas
Located on highway 156 near Larned, KS

Don't Miss!

Heading west on Highway 56, look for signs for Highway 156 going west and turn right on to 156. It's about 6 miles to the entrance to Fort Larned.

Open daily from 8:30 am to 4:30 pm.
Free admission
Ranger guided tours are offered by reservation.
Call (620) 285-6911 for information and reservations.

Mounted Soldier cut-out art at the entrance to Fort Larned. Fort Larned was in service for 19 years, from 1859 to 1878.

Disabled Parking Advantage
The disabled parking spaces are located much closer to the Fort, across a small bridge. Keep following the signs.

Web links for Fort Larned:

http://www.nps.gov/fols/index.htm

http://www.kansastravel.org/fortlarned.htm

The museum is in a former barracks, and has many exhibits, historical photos, and a 10 minute video about Fort History.

🛍️ Gift Shop Alert!

Bookstore Alert - Fort Larned National Historic Site's bookstore contains a wide selection of books about the history and culture of the American West as well as collectibles, clothing, and other memorabilia.

Soldier cut-out art at the entrance to Fort Larned.

This flagpole in the middle of the parade field is 99 feet tall and replaces the original 100 foot flagpole that was destroyed by lighting in 1877.

The Fort's mission originally was to protect the US mail, but their responsibility eventually included protecting travelers on the Santa Fe Trail. The fort closed after the railroad was completed.

Fort Larned is near where the Santa Fe Trail splits into Mountain Branch (or wet route), and Cimarron Cuttoff (or dry route).

69

The bakery made fresh bread for the men stationed at Fort Larned. Wood burning ovens had a large capacity for baking.

Barracks or squad room for the enlisted troops.

Operating table in the doctor's office,.

The carpenter's shop contains tools and workbench. Skilled civilian tradesmen provided services to the Army such as blacksmiths, carpenters, saddlers, and wheelwrights.

View from the jail area looking toward the main part of the fort and parade grounds.

Mary checks out the view from the jail guard shack.

72

Fort Larned was located on the Pawnee River to provide protection from Native Americans and to serve as an escort service along the Santa Fe Trail from 1859 to 1869.

In 1870, the railroad came through central Kansas, and the soldiers provided protection to construction workers.

Mounted Soldier cut-out art at the entrance to Fort Larned.

SF Trail Factoid #49
The 9th and 10th Cavalry regiments were comprised of Black soldiers, who were called 'Buffalo Soldiers' by the Indians, and the nickname has stuck.

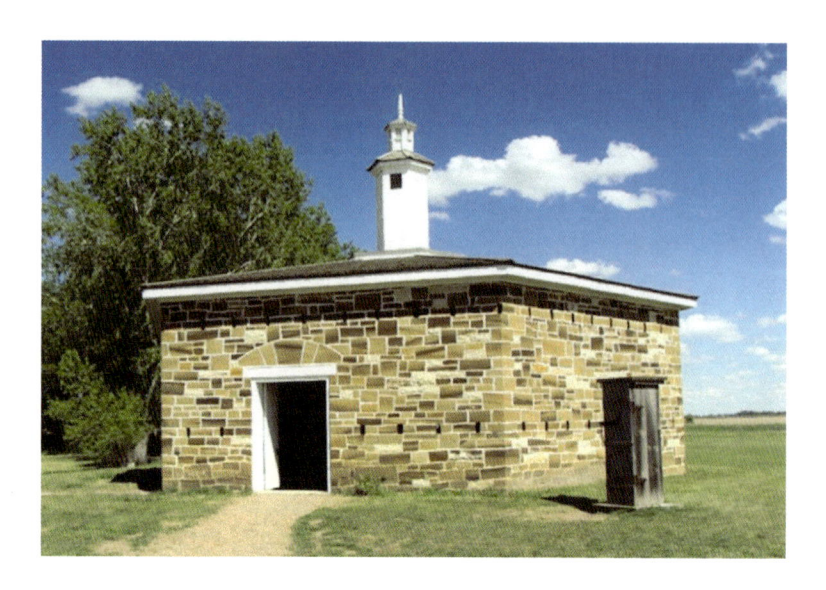

The jail at Fort Larned doesn't have individual cells. There is a hole in the middle where the worst prisoners were kept.

The Block House that served as the jail was originally built for defense, before the rest of the fort was built. Soldiers could fire in any direction thru loopholes in the wall. Over time it was converted to the Post prison. The loopholes were filled in to keep other soldiers from passing libations to their buddies inside. The well in the center was partly filled in and used for solitary confinement.

SF Trail Factoid #48
Sgt. Frank Gibson, Co. D, 19th Infantry, is especially remembered for carving his name into every remaining original stone building at Fort Larned.

Santa Fe Trail Center

Located on Highway 156 between Fort Larned and the community of Larned, is the Santa Fe Trail Center, a locally run museum devoted to the history of the Santa Fe Trail.

Many buildings have been moved to the site including a school house, sod house, and railroad depot. There is also a library and indoor exhibits.

Open 7 days a week in summer. Closed Monday the rest of the year.

Admission to the Santa Fe Trail Center:
$4.00 Adults
$2.50 Students 12-18
$1.50 Children 6-11

Santa Fe Trail Center
Route 3 Box 137
Larned Kansas 67550
(620) 285-2054

SF Trail Factoid #15

A dozen cats were requisitioned by Lt. Henry Heth, the commanding officer of Fort Atkinson, to deal with an infestation of field mice. The Fort was made entirely of sod buildings, which were an attractive home to the mice.

Head west on Highway US 56 after leaving Ft. Larned.

Kinsley, KS is where Highway US 56 and Highway US 50 merge together. Continue traveling west on Highway US 50/56 heading toward Dodge City, KS.

Garfield, Kansas

Named after James A. Garfield, the 20th President of the United States

The Congregational Church built in 1875 was the recipient of a bell given to them by President Garfield.

The Wayside Chapell is a memorial to the first Congregational Church with its cornerstone, and that historic bell. The stone at the base of this marker is the original step to the first church.

Travelers on Highway US 56, passing through Garfield, KS, are invited to pause for prayer to God on life's journey.

Bricks in base of the sign are from the school building erected in 1884 and made in local kiln.

Dodge City, Kansas
http://www.visitdodgecity.org/

Dodge City, KS, was a major crossroad on the Trail, with some of the wagons continuing on west on the Mountain Branch (the wet route) of the trail, and some turning southwest to travel the Cimarron Cutoff (the dry route).

Cut-out art Cowboys welcome travelers to Dodge City.

H.L. Sitler, the first settler of what became Dodge City, said; "If you stood on the hill above Dodge City, there was traffic as far as you could see, 24-hours a day, seven days a week on the Santa Fe Trail."

Fort Dodge opened in 1859 to provide safety from marauding Indians, and protection to wagon trains and the US Mail.

The many attractions in the Dodge City are too numerous to list in this book. (Google Dodge City travel book)

Many national chain hotels/motels are here in Dodge City.

Stay on US 50 and it will go right through the center of Dodge City on US 50.

A few of the Dodge City, KS attractions:

Boot Hill Museum
Front Street & fifth Ave.
(620) 227-8188
www.boothill.org

Carnegie Center for the Arts
Historic building & Art Gallery
701 Second
(620) 225-6388
www.dodgecityarts.org

Dodge City Roundup Rodeo
Rodeo Events
608 S. 14th
(620) 225-2244
www.dodgecityroundup.org

Santa Fe Depot & Mexican Village Marker
Once housed the Harvey House Hotel & Restaruant
Wyatt Earp & Central Ave.
(620) 225-1001
www.depottheatreco.com

Visitor's Information Center & Historic Trolley Tours
Self-guided walking and driving tours & Trolley Tours available
400 W. Wyatt Earp
1-800-OLD-WEST
www.visitdodgecity.org

Old Dodge Photo Parlor
Old Tyme Photos
214 ½ West Wyatt Earp
(620) 225-2929

Dodge City Zoo
South 2nd, Wright Park
(620) 225-8163
www.dodgecityroundup.org

Fort Dodge
Historic 1800s Fort & Museum
E. Hwy 400
(620) 227-2121
www.kansasfrontierforts.com

Santa Fe Trail Tracks, US Survey Team

9 miles West of Doge City
Highway 50/400
Ph: (620) 227-8188

Near the present site of Dodge City Kansas the trail splits. The more commonly used branch continued up the north bank of the Arkansas River to Bent's Old Fort, between the present towns of Las Animas and La Junta, CO. From this point the trail turned southwest to Trinidad, CO, pulled its way over Raton Pass, and on to Santa Fe, NM.

Lois and Mary approach the information kiosk at U.S. Survey site. The terrain continues to be gently undulating prairie.

The sign says:
Camping near this location Sept. 10, 1825, the survey team remained through September 21 waiting for a courier with information from the U.S. Government as how to proceed further. West of the 100th meridian which surveyor Joseph Brown had mistakenly identified as being at this point and south of the Arkansas river was Mexican territory where the survey team has no permission to enter. Receiving no such information, the team divided with commissioner George Sibley, surveyor Brown, interpreter William Williams, nine men and Sibley's servant Abram continuing on with the survey. The other two commissioners, Benjamin Reeves and Thomas Mather with secretary Archibald Gamble and the rest of the team returned to Missouri.

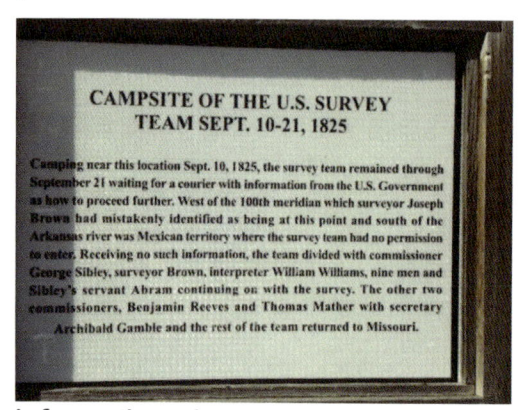

Cimarron, Kansas

🛏 **Cimarron Crossing Bed & Breakfast**,
owned and operated by Gerald and Joan Vogel
307 West Ave. A, Cimarron, KS 67835
620-855-3030 or 888-829-3232
www.cimarroncrossing.com

🍴 No restaurants in this town, so plan ahead.

SF Trail Factoid #9
The route to the Cimarron River was often without water, and this section of the trail was known as 'La Jornada del Muerte' or 'The Journey of Death'

81

There is a tornado shelter in the back yard; we don't see too many of those in California.

Country Kitchen with fire-burning stove and oven.

82

We were served a delicious, hearty homemade breakfast of quiche, fresh fruit, juice, and coffee.

All of the guest bedrooms have themes: Santa Fe, Missouri, Arizona, and West Texas.

Innkeeper Joan Vogel and Lois at entrance to Cimarron Crossing Bed & Breakfast.

We decided to take the Mountain Branch instead of the Cimarron Cutoff, because we wanted to see Bent's Fort, Trinidad, and Raton Pass.

SF Trail Factoid #59

When a mule pulling the mail wagon would get sick on the road, the men would take care of him by putting a blanket on, and leaving him at watering hole with a sack of corn thrown on the ground. On the return trip, sometimes the mule would still be there, or he would die or stray away, or Indians would take him. Sometimes the Indians would take a sick mule and then give him back on the return trip.

Charlie's Ruts
– best rut's in Lois's opinion.

Located 4 miles east of Lakin, KS, on Highway 50 is a fine set of parallel ruts ascending a hill to the east. Look for them on the north side of the highway and marked with a Kansas State Historical Society marker.

Becky at gate to Charlie's Ruts

Mailbox at Charlie's Ruts. There is a notebook inside that you can sign if you want to.

SF Trail Factoid #43

A trading post known as Barclay's Fort served as headquarters of a Mr. Kroenig, who used camels to pack merchandise on the Trail.

This sign explains how to know when you see a rut.

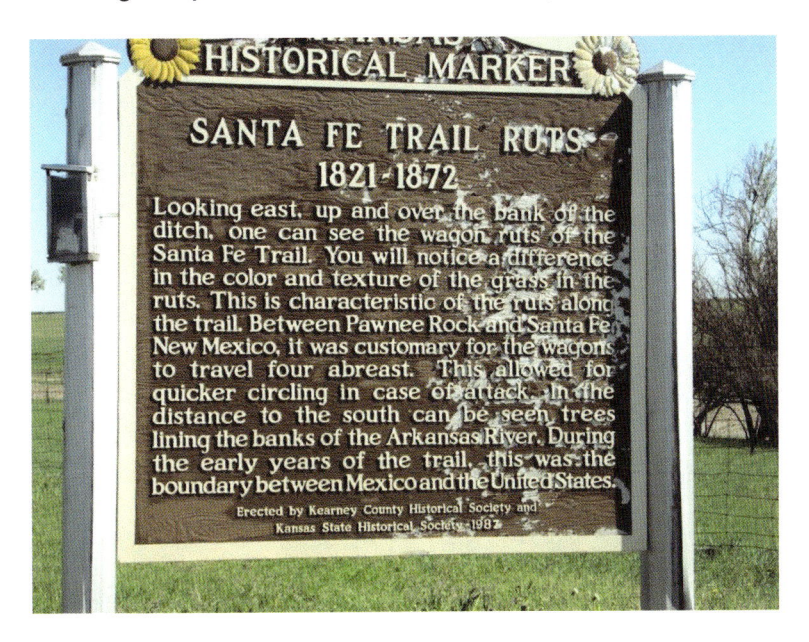

The sign says:

"Looking east, up and over the bank of the ditch, one can see the wagon ruts of the Santa Fe Trail. You will notice a difference in the color and texture of the grass in the ruts. This is characteristic of the ruts along the trail. Between Pawnee rock and Santa Fe, New Mexico, it was customary for the wagons to travel four abreast. This allowed for quicker circling in case of attack. In the distance to the south can be seen trees lining the banks for the Arkansas River. During the early years of the trail, this was the boundary between Mexico and the United States."

SF Trail Factoid #8
The Santa Fe Trail follows the valley of the Arkansas River through much of western Kansas.

Look !! There's some actual ruts!

A wagon rut is visible in the sandy soil on the slope of the hill.

SF Trail Factoid #41

There were old sailors who believed it would be possible to build a sailing wagon to travel the road to Santa Fe, freeing freighters from the need for draft animals. The most famous was 'WindWagon Thomas', who constructed an experimental vessel. Unfortunately, it crashed on it's maiden voyage.

Lakin, Kansas

On Highway 50, between Cimarron, KS and Lamar, CO.

Grain storage that is next to the Kearney County Museum. We saw many of these grain storage facilities as we travelled through Kansas, reminding us that we were in America's breadbasket.

The Kearney County Museum complex is located 6 blocks south of US Highway 50, at the corner of Buffalo and Waterman.

Welcome to Kearny Co Museum!
Open 9 to 12, 1 to 4, Tuesday to Friday.
Open Sunday 1 to 4.

Folksy little museum that contains

87

artifacts from the founding families of Kearny County, ranging from dishware, household goods, family portraits, to wagons, saddles, and artwork.

The museum complex consists of the museum building and annex, the White House, the School House, Santa Fe Depot, Farm Machinery building and the Round Barn, totaling over 20,000 square feet of historical displays.

The main museum building has a wide variety of displays such as turn-of-the-century (1900) parlor, dining room, and kitchen with furniture, china and linins that were typical of the period. There is a Conestoga wagon, ingenious furniture such as the bookshelf that converts to a dining table, musical instruments, and bronze statues. An aerial composite photograph of the Lakin area shows the Arkansas River and old Trail travel routes.

Lois inside the Kearny County Museum, admiring the covered wagon.

88

The Kearney County Museum has a Conestoga Wagon in it's collection that bears the inscription "Joseph Edgar – 1831". This wagon does not have a seat in it because all the space was taken up by goods for sale. The men walked alongside of and slept under the wagon.

Items in the museum include this beautiful bronze horse.

SF Trail Factoid #60

In early mail service days, there were 2 sacks of mail – the 'through sack' that was not opened until Santa Fe, and the 'way sack' containing mail for the stations along the route. When the mail wagon reached a station, the 'way sack' would be dumped on the floor, and people would look through the pile and take what belonged to them. The rest would continue down the road.

Drawing of how the wagons traveled four abreast, and not in single file.

The Historic Lakin Train Station is next to the Kearney County Museum.

The Santa Fe depot was built in 1876 to replace a boxcar that was used as a station first. The town of Lakin, KS, rallied together to raise money to save the station from demolition in 1982, and turned it into a museum.

SF Trail Factoid #18
On average, a caravan traveled 15 miles a day.

SF Trail Factoid #39
Most of the DAR markers erected along the Santa Fe Trail in the early 1900s cost $16 apiece.

Gas prices in Lakin, KS, May 2010

SF Trail Factoid #21
The major reason the Mountain Branch was promoted was because the Cimarron Cutoff was unsafe due to hostile threats from the Kiowa and Comanche.

Lamar, Colorado

Located at the corner of Main and Beech streets in Lamar, CO, the Madonna of the Trail statue is near the Colorado Welcome Center, as shown in this picture.

Incised on the base:

"NSDAR Memorial to the Pioneer Mothers of the Covered Wagon Days.
"In Commemoration of the 'Big Timbers' extending eastward and westward along the Arkansas river approximately twenty mile east of Bent's new Fort, later Fort Wise, 1832 – 1832

"A place of historical lore noted for Indian lodges; shelter from storm and heat; food supply for beast; bivouac for expeditions; scene of many councils."

The Big Timbers was a long belt of gigantic cottonwoods growing along the Arkansas River where the valley widened.

The trees stood along a buffalo migratory route and were a welcome site to Native Americans, pioneers, army units, and traders.

The grove of cottonwoods was considered so significant to the history of the area that this spot was chosen by the Daughters of the American Revolution as the location for the National Madonna of the Trail Monument

A Belgian draft horse grazes in a pasture next to Highway 50. Draft animals were invaluable to early settlers, and were often crossed with a donkey to produce draft mules, such as the mule in the corral at Bent's Fort.

SF Trail Factoid #36
Three Pioneer Mother statues, erected by the DAR, are located along the Santa Fe Trail in Lexington, MO, Council Grove, KS, and Lamar, CO

The Bent County Courthouse is a majestic brick building located in the middle of Las Animas, Colorado.

725 Carson Avenue
Las Animas, CO 81054
(719) 456-1600

Built in 1886-89, this two-story red brick building is the oldest courthouse in continuous use in Colorado. Many of the original courthouse furnishings are still in use today.

Also in the area:
- Kit Carson Museum
- 1902 Jail near the Courthouse
- Old Trail Art Gallery by the only stop light in Las Animas
- Fort Lyon Kit Carson Chapel (5 miles east of Las Animas), Boggsville (south of Las Animas).

Bent's Fort, Colorado
Bent's Old Fort National Historic Site
35110 highway 194 East
La Junta, CO 81050-9523
719-383-5010
www.nps.gov/beol

Don't miss the video about the history of Bent's Fort, which is located eight miles east of La Junta, CO on Highway 194, and preserves the site and the story of a famous trading post.

Approaching Bent's Fort on the trail from the parking lot. Don't be shy about using the phone in the parking lot to call for a ride, it's farther than it looks.

Gift Shop Alert!
Excellent Gift shop with historic items and low prices.

95

Bent's Old Fort was one of the significant centers of fur trade on the Santa Fe Trail, influencing economies around the world. Built by brothers Charles and William Bent and their business partner Ceran St. Vrain in 1833, the fort was the leading industry west of the Mississippi in the early 1830s. For 16 years, Bent, St. Vrain and Co. managed a prosperous trading empire. The Fort was located on an established road, it helped pave the way for the occupation of the west by the U.S. Army, and was an instrument of Manifest Destiny and the invasion of Mexico in 1846.

Typical good changing hands in the trade room included beaver pelts and buffalo robes, powder horns, tobacco, cloth and blankets, pipes, gunpowder, tools, dried foods, bells, and beads.

SF Trail Factoid #56

In 1840, Bielzy Dodd, a trapper friend of William Bent, walked among the Indians camped around Ft. William eyeing them savagely. With a terrifying yell, he pulled off his wig and threw it on the ground before the horrified Indians, who thereafter called him 'the white-man-who-scalps-himself'.

96

The Starts and Strips flying over Bent's Fort.

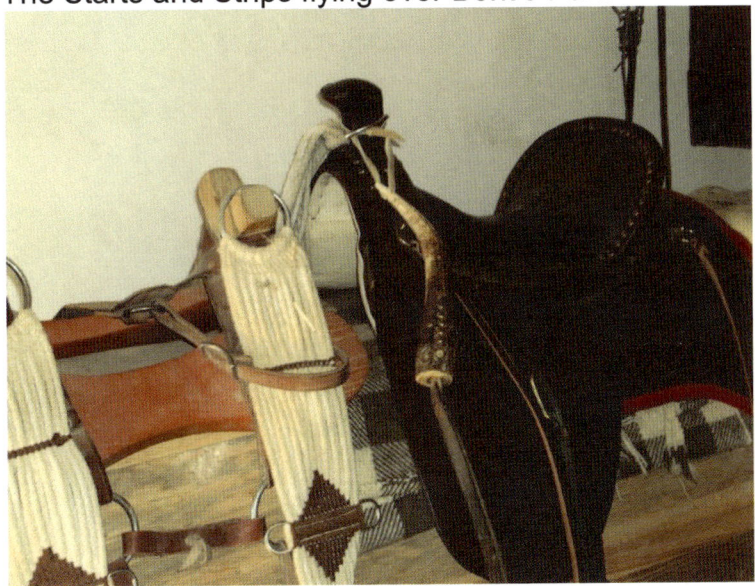

Examples of pack saddle and riding saddle from the era.

Kitchen storage; well what do you expect from the far West in the 1850s? Built-in storage cabinets?

Lois enjoys the peace and quiet, while Becky and Mary explore the Fort.

98

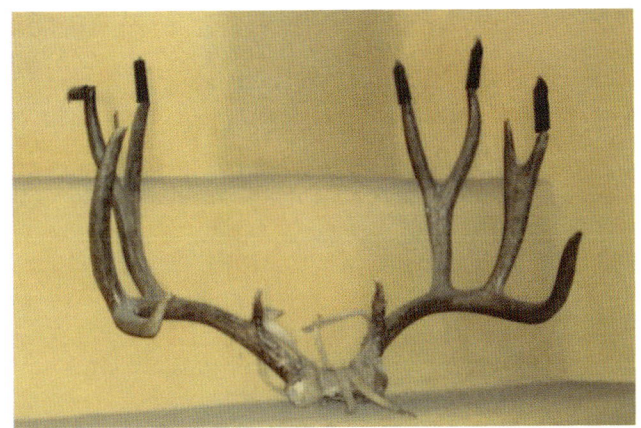

There is a Bar upstairs in the Fort, with familiar bar accoutrements like these antlers used as a candelabra.

Fully stocked bar here at the Fort, must have been one of the most popular 'watering holes' for miles around.

View from the southern wall of Bent's Fort, up on the roof, looking toward the Arkansas River, which is visible in the left part of the photo as a blue pool.

The corral at Bent's Fort is home to peacocks and mules.

The easy way to get back to the parking lot. The friendly driver gives us a ride back to our vehicle, with Lois enjoying the front seat view, and Mary with her bags of treasures from the gift store.

SF Trail Factoid #20
In 1845, the famous army explorer John C. Fremont traveled westward from Bent's Fort to California.

La Junta, Colorado

After leaving Bent's Fort, head west on highway 194 towards La Junta, CO.

La Junta is Spanish for The Junction, and is where the Santa Fe Trail and the Navajo Trail part ways.

La Junta Local Sights

Koshare Indian Museum – Plains Indian art and artifacts and Koshare Kiva Dances.
115 W. 18th Street, La Junta, CO 384-4411

Otero Museum – Old store, blacksmith shop, stage coach house, log cabin school and boarding house, exhibits and artifacts of Santa Fe Trail era.
3rd and Anderson, 384-7406

Santa Fe Railroad Plaza
Highway 50 and Santa Fe Avenue
Interpreted downtown park provides visitors a look at La Junta history with an old railroad car, kiosk with visitor information and picnic tables in downtown La Junta.

Court House Square – Santa Fe Trail DAR marker #17 dedicated in 1906 in downtown La Junta. Marker 17 is on the southeast corner of La Junta's Court House Square facing south. On Colorado 194 go west to La Junta. Turn south and cross the Arkansas River bridge. The Santa Fe Trail crossed to the south side of the river about six miles west of Bent's Old Fort, near present La Junta.

Felisa's Mexican Food & Lounge
27948 Frontage Rd, La Junta, CO 81050
(719) 384-4814

Several nation chain motels such as Holiday Inn, Super 8, Travel Inn, Hampton Inn

Local Hotels such as Stagecoach, La Junta Inn and Suites, Midtown Motel

Bent's Fort Gift Shop sells jars of Scaff Brothers salsa, green chili, and hot sauce. Headquartered in La Juanta, CO, Scaff Brothers make salsa, BBQ sauce, steak sauce, Piqueoso sauce, and a whole passel of other products that can be purchased from their website.

http://www.scaffbros.com/

"Taste of the Country" Products like fruit cobblers and preserves, Jalapeño Honey Mustard, fruit butters, and pickled vegetables like watermelon rind and sweet fire pickles.

I just love edible souvenirs from my travels!

Metal cut-out signs are popular in this area. Here is a fine example of a Bull Sign

SF Trail Factoid #72

The origin of the Arkansas River is in the Rocky Mountains in Lake County, Colorado, near Leadville. In 1859 placer gold was discovered in the Leadville area bringing thousands seeking to strike it rich, however the easily recovered placer gold was quickly exhausted.

On the Road – Highway 350

Leaving La Junta, CO heading for Trinidad, CO, we turn south on Highway 350.

Cruise down Highway 350 after leaving La Junta, traveling in a southerly direction towards Trinidad. We are at a higher elevation now, and the terrain is changing from fields of wheat to flat grazing lands.

We are starting to see more hills and rocky terrain, like this mesa. Note the high desert plants instead of the grassy prairie.

Iron Spring Historic Area.

27 miles south of La Junta, CO on Highway 350, turn left at County Road 9 and drive 1 mile to the parking lot.

Iron Springs was an important water stop for travelers on the Santa Fe Trail. Between 1861 and 1871, Iron Spring was used as a stage coach station. An important water supply on the trail, it was the scene of several Indian attacks. Trail ruts are visible near the spring west of the parking lot, and a few ruins remain nearby.

Santa Fe Trail Marker at Iron Spring Historic Area.

SF Trail Factoid #84
When newly appointed governor Don Pedro de Peralta chose Santa Fe as the capital of the Spanish Kingdom of New Mexico in 1610, he changed the name of the city to La Villa Real de Santa Fe de San Francisco de Asis – the Royal City of the Holy Faith of St. Francis of Assisi.

The sign says:
"We marched at the usual hour – 7am and at a distance of 13 miles we found a large water hole and boiling spring.the taste of Iron in the Spring is very strong…Deep trails of Antelope and deer lead to lead to the Spring from every point of the Compass."

John Pope, 1851

Becky and Lois read the historical marker Pasaron Por Aqui (The Trail passed by here.) at Iron Spring Historic Area.

As traders made their way back and forth along the Trail, the wheels of their wagons and the hooves of their oxen and mules cut into the earth, leaving behind distinctive depressions, the remains of which we still see today. Rainfall naturally collects in these ruts, stimulating plant growth. Today, the relatively high concentration of plants in the trail ruts creates ribbons of vegetation that wind across the plains.

Pinon Canyon Maneuver Site

It seemed out of place to see an Army tank parked off on the east side of Highway US 325, at the entrance to Pinon Canyon Maneuver Site.

The Army purchased the land making up Pinon Canyon Maneuver Site in 1983. Eminent domain was used to acquire almost half the area as many land owners were unwilling sellers. The purpose of PCMS is "to provide critical maneuver lands" for soldiers from Fort Carson and other military bases.

SF Trail Factoid #61
The mail service contractors had a corral at Council Grove with about 100 mules. The mail wagons would pick out fresh mules before continuing down the Santa Fe Trail.

Indian rock paintings on display at the Pinon Canyon Maneuver Site.

The army won't let you go out into the canyon to see the Indian rock paintings, but they have some on display in their headquarters building.

Prior to the creation of PCMS this area was lightly populated and devoted almost entirely to ranching and livestock grazing. A branch of the Santa Fe Trail runs near PCMS and ancient Indian rock art and petroglyphs are common in the rocky canyons. Pronghorn, Elk, and Mule Deer are the principal large mammals found in the area.

View from Pinion Canyon Maneuver Site of Sangre de Cristo Mountains, with Spanish Peaks on the right.

SF Trail Factoid #50
Known as Wah-to-Yah and the Breasts of the Earth, the Spanish Peaks were visible to Trail travelers on the Mountain Branch for great distances.

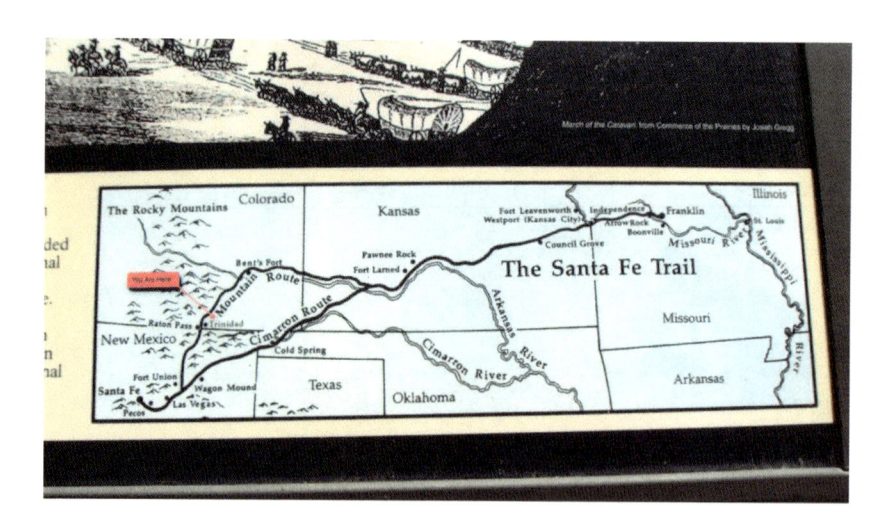

The now-familiar map of the historical Santa Fe Trail. Look how far we have come! Almost to Santa Fe.

110

High Desert Landscapes

Cattle are in a pasture in the high desert next to Highway 350. The terrain continues to become more mountainous.

Fisher's Peak (9,627) from a distance, as we approach Trinidad. It's a very prominent, visible landmark that was used by Trail travelers.

SF Trail Factoid #29
The record horseback ride, from Santa Fe to Independence, was made by Francis X. Aubry in 5 days and 22 hours.

Trinidad, Colorado

On Highway 25, in Colorado, just north of Raton Pass.

Colorado State Welcome Center
309 Nevada, Trinidad, CO
(719) 846-9512   www.historictrinidad.com

View of **Fisher's Peak** (9,627) on east side of town as we arrive in Trinidad, CO, which has mountain peaks on both sides of town.

The Trinidad Trolley offers free tours hourly from 10am to 3pm every day, Memorial Day through Labor Day and Saturdays in winter, weather permitting. The trolley stops at the Welcome Center and all the museums. For private group reservations winter or summer call (719) 846-9843 x33.

SF Trail Factoid #28
The famous landmark Fisher's Peak (aka Raton Peak) overlooks the northern entrance to Raton Pass.

As you enter Trinidad, **Simpson's Rest** (6,462) is on west side.

A historic sandstone bluff, Simpson's Rest, stands at Trinidad's northern limits. The mountain has the Trinidad sign which lights up the evening skies and serves as a beacon to modern day trail travelers. The bluff, overlooking the town from the north can be reached by way of a road leading from the western end of North Avenue.

SF Trail Factoid #80
Santa Fe was once the site of Pueblo Indian villages that seem to have been abandoned centuries before the Spanish arrived in 1607.

🛍 Gift Shop Alert!
Best shopping on the Trail so far.
We enjoyed window shopping in Trinidad, CO, and looking at the artistic woven blankets and paintings.

What a beautufil variety of treasures! The bright colors are a welcome contrast to the dusty trail.

114

The First National Bank Building was erected in 1892

The bank is on the main street running through Trinidad, along the route of the actual Santa Fe Trail. This is the cash register from a local store, a reminder of the old days. And it's beautiful to look at.

115

Tarabino Inn
310 E. 2nd Street
Trinidad, Colorado 81082
http://www.tarabinoinn.com
866-846-8808

We arrived early, and were warmly welcomed with warm cookies, tea, and coffee. In the morning we were served a full homemade breakfast before continuing down the Santa Fe Trail..

Tarabino Inn is a certified historical structure.

View of sunset taken from the second floor of Tarabino Inn.

Nana & Nano's Pasta House – Fine Italian Food
418 East Main Street
Trinidad, Colorado 81082
(719) 846-2629
Dine with Us or Take it Out

Monteleone's Deli – Food to Go
Owned and Managed by Fran Monteleone, shares the space with Nana's. Locals eat here; it was packed.
- Imported & Domestic Cheeses
- Fine Meats
- Cold Cuts
- Party Trans
- Homemade Sandwiches

Mary says: 'Loved the peanut brittle with chili mixed in, red or green, it was spicy and delicious!'

Bella Luna Pizzeria – Dine In or Take Out
121 W. Main St.
Trinidad, CO 81082
(719) 846-2750

Open: Monday – Saturday 11am – 3pm for lunch
5pm – 9pm for Dinner
Sunday 12pm – 6pm
Closed Tuesdays

Becky says: Great pizza!

Back on the Trail, heading out of Trinidad, going south toward Raton Pass, we take a last photo of Fisher's Peak at the corner of Santa Fe Trail and Moores Canyon Road.

A.R. Mitchell Museum & Gallery

150 E. Main Street
Trinidad, Colorado 81082

Open May – September, 10am – 4pm, Tuesday thru Sunday
Admission is charged (for non-members)
Call for off-season hours – (719) 846-4224

An extraordinary collection of Spanish colonial folk art is on display.

The museum has a permanent collection of over 350 original paintings by acclaimed western artist Arthur Roy Mitchell and his contemporaries. There is also a collection of historic photographs and cameras on display

The A.R. Mitchell Museum gift shop and fine art gallery is open year-round and carries prints of paintings in the museum and original works by local artists.

SF Trail Factoid #34
The Trail must pass through the Sangre de Cristo mountain range to reach Santa Fe, via Raton Pass.

Trinidad History Museum

300 E. Main Street
Trinidad, Colorado 81082
(719) 846-7217

Admission is charged (for non-members)
Open May 1 – September 30 every day
Tours begin at 10am; last tour leaves at 4pm.
Group tours by reservation October – April.
www.coloradohistory.org

The grounds are home to the Santa Fe Trail Museum, the Baca House, and the Bloom Mansion.

Don't miss the Trinidad History Museum gift store located around the corner on Main Street, filled with books such as "Land of Enchantment" and "Quest for Quivira", a bog of old buttons, handmade Indian Christmas ornaments.

Beautiful soap bars are decorated with dried flowers and ribbon and make nice gifts for your loved ones at home.

Colorful flowers brighten the streets of Trinidad, CO.

Highway 25 heading South.

Sangre de Cristo Mountains (14,000) display their white ribbon of snow capping the dark mountains.

Spanish Peaks are in sharp focus now, West Peak (13,626) and East Peak (12,683).

Look how much the terrain has changed from Kansas. This beautiful landscape is in southern Colorado, just leaving Trinidad heading towards Raton Pass.

SF Trail Factoid #24
It could take up to a week to travel thru the Raton Pass, while the modern traveler takes an hour.

Raton Pass

Welcome to New Mexico, the Land of Enchantment. The elevation at Raton Pass is 7,834 feet.

Coming out of Raton Pass into New Mexico, driving south on Highway 25, we see this view of Sierra Grande (8,720) in the distance in the middle of the photo and Laughlin Peak (8,818) in the distance on the right.

Here is an artist's rendering of how Raton Pass used to look. And this was after improvements were made for the railroad.

SF Trail Factoid #23

Raton Pass was described by a traveler in 1847 as very steep, awful for wagons, and almost nothing but rocks. The travelers rejoiced when they reached the bottom of the last hill in safety.

SF Trail Factoid #14

Raton Pass took five days to cross, with many wagons being wrecked during the 27 mile trek.

Raton, New Mexico
On Highway 25, heading South

Modern day Raton, NM, is a small town on the high desert, with shops, restaurants, hotels, and gas stations.

SF Trail Factoid #25
'Uncle Dick' Wootton made improvements to the Raton Pass road in 1865, and charged a toll of $1.50 per wagon.

SF Trail Factoid #26
All Trail travelers and loose livestock were charged to use 'Uncle Dick's' toll road, but Indians were allowed to use the road for free.

Look at the price of Gas in 2010!

124

Raton's electric sign on the top of Goat Hill. The top can be reached by car.

'Uncle Dick' Wootton sold the rights to the toll road to the Santa Fe Railroad in 1879. The railroad ordered a gargantuan locomotive to conquer the steep 6 percent grade, and named it the 'Uncle Dick'.

It was so heavy it had to be shipped in pieces for assembly in Trinidad, CO, and was the world's largest engine of its time, weighing 150,000 pounds.

Other sights nearby - Capulin Volcano

Capulin Volcano National Monument
PO Box 40
Capulin, NM 88414
(575) 278-2201

www.nps.gov/cavo

There is an entrance fee of $5 per vehicle.

Capulin Volcano National Monument is 30 miles east of Raton. Turn east on Highway 64/87 and drive until you get to the town of Capulin, then turn north on N.Mex. 325 for about 3 miles to the park entrance.

Gift Shop Alert!

At the Visitor Center at the base of the volcano, you will pay the entrance fee and find information, a book store, and exhibits, plus a 10 minute film about Capulin volcano and the immense power of volcanoes.

Bring a picnic lunch and enjoy the view from the summit. There is also a picnic area near the Visitor Center with water and restrooms.

There is a parking lot on the summit (bless them!), and various hiking trails.

- **Crater Rim Trail** – a one mile long paved trail goes around the rim of the volcano, offering spectacular view of the surrounding high plains. The trail skirts the rim in a series of moderate to steep ascents to the peak's highest point – 8,182 feet – and ends with a steep descent to the parking lot. Sounds like a nice hike, but not with my arthritis.

- **Crater Vent Trail** – steeply descends 105 feet to the bottom of the crater, the plugged vent of Capulin volcano. For the very curious who don't mind the 105 very steep climb back up to the parking lot.

- A 10 minute **Nature Trail** begins at the visitor center. Paved and wheelchair-accessible, it offers close-up view of the prairie landscape and lava formations called squeeze-ups. Sounds like a winner.

- **Lava Flow Trail** is a one mile loop that begins at the far end of the visitor center parking lot. There are some steep sections and rugged lava exposed on this otherwise easy, unpaved trail. Sounds like a mixed bag, let the rambunctious travelers go for it and stretch their muscles out.

- **Boca Trail** is a strenuous two mile unimproved loop trail across lava flows, with lava lakes, lava tubes, and a spatter hill along the way. If anyone has been feeling too cooped up in the car, send them out on this trail while the rest of you enjoy the picnic lunch.

Highway 25 into New Mexico

View of the **Turkey Mountains** (7,877) from Highway 25, driving over the arid high desert. The rock layers are made of beautiful bands of color.

We are now closer to **Laughlin Peak** (8,818 ft), and headed straight for it. The terrain has scattered mountains and volcanoes now.

View of snow-capped **Sangre de Cristo Mountains** (12,000). There is not as much snow on the peaks here, since they are not as tall as the northern part of the mountain range.

Wagon Mound

This rock formation was an important landmark since it can been seen in the distance and is easy to recognize.

We could see Wagon Mound a long way away. There is a small town there now.

SF Trail Factoid #51

Wagon Mound is a famous Trail landmark that received its name because it looks like a Wagon when viewed from a distance.

SF Trail Factoid #52

The Wagon Mound Massacre occurred in 1850 when an east-bound stagecoach was attacked by Jicarilla Apache and Ute Indians, killing all 10 passengers.

Ft Union National Monument

Look for exit 366 at Watrous, NM from Highway 25, and then it's about 8 miles to Fort Union on NM-161.

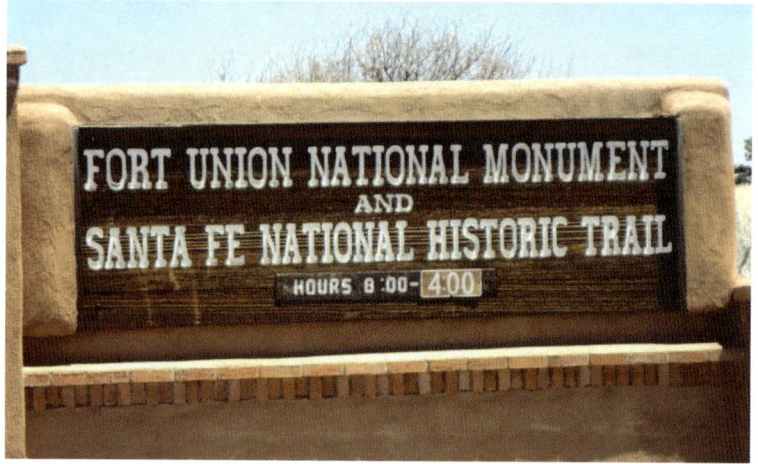

Open daily except Thanksgiving Day, Christmas Day, and New Year's Day.

Winter: Labor Day to Memorial Day 8:00 am to 4:00 pm.
Summer: Memorial Day to Labor Day 8:00 am to 6:00 pm

The two branches of the Santa Fe Trail – the Mountain Branch and the Cimarron Cutoff – converge again just beyond Fort Union.

"Many ladies greatly dislike Fort Union. It has always been noted for severe dust storms. Situated on a barren plain, the nearest mountains…three miles distant, it has the most exposed position of any military fort in New Mexico…The hope of having any trees, or even a grassy parade-ground, had been abandoned long before our residence there….Every eye is said to form it's own beauty. Mine was disposed to see much in Fort Union, for I had a home there." Mrs. Orsemus B. Boyd, 1984, recalling her residence at Fort Union in 1872.

🛍️ Gift Shop Alert!

Three recipes from 'Authentic INDIAN – MEXICAN Recipes' are reprinted in this book.

SF Trail Factoid #2
During the Mexican war, the Trail was also used by the American Army.

Fort Union had the premier hospital in the region with six wards and thirty-six beds. Treatment and care was available for fifty cents per day.

The third re-construction of Fort Union, whose ruins are there today, took six years to complete. The sprawling installation was the most extensive in the territory, and included not only a military post, but a separate quartermaster depot with warehouses, corrals, shops, officers, and quarters. The supply function overshadowed that of the military and employed far more men, mostly civilians.

The supply depot flourished until 1879, when the Santa Fe Railroad replaced the Santa Fe Trail as the principal avenue of commerce. By 1891 the fort had outlived its usefulness and was abandoned.

During the 1860s and 1870s, troops from Fort Union were involved in wars against the Apaches, Navajos, Cheyenne, Arapahos, Kiowas, Utes and Comanches.

Peace was achieved in the spring of 1875, and the Fort's garrison turned to other roles such as helping to track down outlaws, quell mob violence, and mediate feuds.

SF Trail Factoid #42

Fort Union, in New Mexico, remained in active service after the Santa Fe Trail was replaced by the railroad.

Fort Union Hospital Ruins

The hospital as it looked shortly after being built.

Hospital ruins today. It's a harsh environment with lots of wind, which has worn down the buildings.

SF Trail Factoid #47
The Battle of Glorietta Pass has been called the Gettysburg of the West, because of the significance as the turning point of the war in the region.

133

Lois and Mary enjoy exploring the paths at Fort Union, on a typically windy day. It's colder than it was in Kansas, too.

This sign shows that the Santa Fe Trail cuts through Fort Union at this exact spot.

134

There are wagon ruts out there somewhere.

We pass the Santa Fe Trail Marker as we leave Fort Union, and resume our journey to Santa Fe! Almost there, but by wagon train, a few more days travel.

Highway 25 – Glorietta Pass

Cruising down Highway 25 toward Glorietta Pass, it's hard to imagine the wagon trains traveling from Independence, MO crawling along rocky, primitive roads.

Its smooth driving through Glorietta Pass these days.

Thompson Peak, elevation 10,554 feet. It doesn't look that high after the dramatic increase in height from the valley floor of the Rocky Mountains. But it is. See the Elevation Chart on page 145.

Santa Fe, New Mexico

The Plaza in Santa Fe, NM, we reached our destination!

The Palace of the Governors on the north side of Santa Fe Plaza once served as the seat of government for the Spanish colony of Neuvo Mexico, and later the state of New Mexico.

SF Trail Factoid #12
The Palace of Governors on Santa Fe Plaza is the oldest non-Indian public structure still in use in the United States.

Native Americans sell beautiful handmade jewelry and artwork on the sidewalk in front of the Palace of the Governors. Copper bracelets, turquoise and silver, kachinas, pottery, and earrings are just the start.

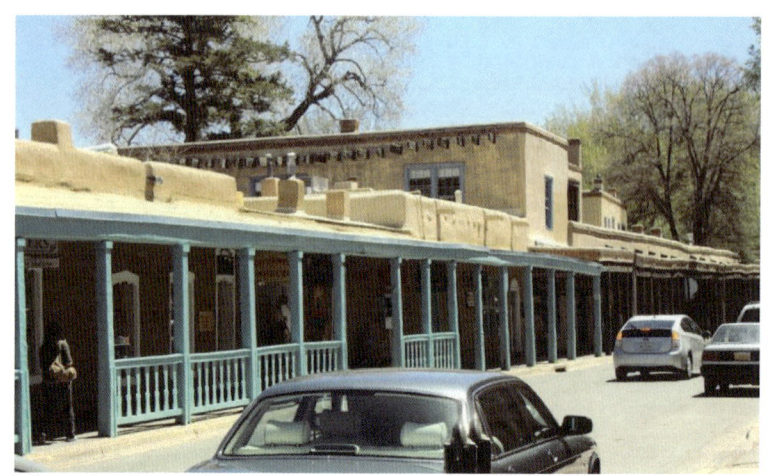

Historic Sena Plaza is just down the street from the Palace of the Governors. It once was part of the rambling Sena family compound.

The Plaza is the center of Santa Fe, surrounded by shops, art galleries, and historic buildings. Vendors sell food and artists offer their paintings in the open air of the Plaza.

Bright watercolor painting created by a local artist, who was selling her wares on the edge of the park.

Turquoise jewelry is for sale in many of the shops on Santa Fe Square. Each turquoise mine has unique coloring and veins; this pair of earrings is on the green side of the color pallet, as opposed to blue.

One-of-a-kind basket is carved out of a single piece of wood and was found at an open air bazaar just south of the La Fonda Hotel. No way to get this into my luggage, it's a carry-on for sure.

SF Trail Factoid #55
Custom duties in 1825 were 25% of the value of the goods. In later years, the fees were assessed at so much per wagon - regardless of cargo – and ranged from $500 to $950 for each wagon. Traders started to consolidate the goods in the wagons before they reached the customs officials, to reduce the number of wagons actually going into Santa Fe, thus reducing fees paid.

The La Fonda Hotel

100 E. San Francisco, Santa Fe, New Mexico 87501
(800) 523-5002   www.lafondasantafe.com

We treated ourselves to a few days in this historic and beautiful hotel at the actual end of the Santa Fe Trail. (Thanks, Mom!)

La Fonda Hotel is on the Old Santa Fe Trail & Route 66!

Lois on the second floor of La Fonda. We are in this grand hotel after traveling 800 miles across the Kansas prairie, the Colorado high plains, and the New Mexico high desert. We slept well that night.

Beautiful iron gates in a hallway in La Fonda Hotel, leading to our room on the second floor.

SF Trail Factoid #30
The Santa Fe Trail does not end in Santa Fe, but connects with El Camino Real, or the Chihuahua Trail

This famous landmark hotel is the latest hotel to be built on this site in the Pueblo Revival style. After its completion in 1922, it was a popular destination for the rich and famous, and still retains its authentic charm and glamour.

141

The entrance to the La Fonda Hotel, is seen from the Plaza, at the corner of Old Santa Fe Trail, and San Francisco.

For the Santa Fe's most impressive sunsets, take the elevator up to the Bell Tower Bar for cocktails during the warm-weather months. The tower faces west, and looks out over the city.

The La Fonda Hotel

SF Trail Factoid #81

As Santa Fe grew, the Spanish colonists used the Pueblo method of adobe construction for their churches, homes, and government buildings. The adobe kept the homes warm in winter and cool in summer. Mud-brick fireplaces and outdoor ovens were popular additions.

A view of Loretto Chapel from the La Fonda.

View from La Fonda Hotel looking east, towards the Sange De Christo mountain range. The view towards the west looks over the city of Santa Fe.

The authors – Becky, Lois, and Mary – at La Plazuela restaurant on the first floor of the La Fonda Hotel.

La Plazuela Restaurant
Call 505.995.2334 for reservations.

Breakfast: 7:00 a.m. – 11:30 am daily
Lunch: Monday – Friday 11:30 am – 2:00 pm
       Saturday & Sunday 11:30 am – 3:00 pm
Dinner: 5:30 pm – 10:00 pm daily

La Plazuela dining room is filled with natural light and whimsical folk art touches, like the legendary hand-painted windows. The menu ranges from American classic dishes to Northern New Mexico specialties. Something for everyone – beef, chicken, pork, lamb, fish, and vegetarian.

SF Trail Factoid #33
The Treaty of Guadalupe Hidalgo, signed by Mexico and the United States in 1848, ceded much of the American Southwest to the United States.

Elevation Chart

This chart shows the change in elevation from Franklin, Missouri to Santa Fe, New Mexico.

Elevation of Points on the Santa Fe Trail

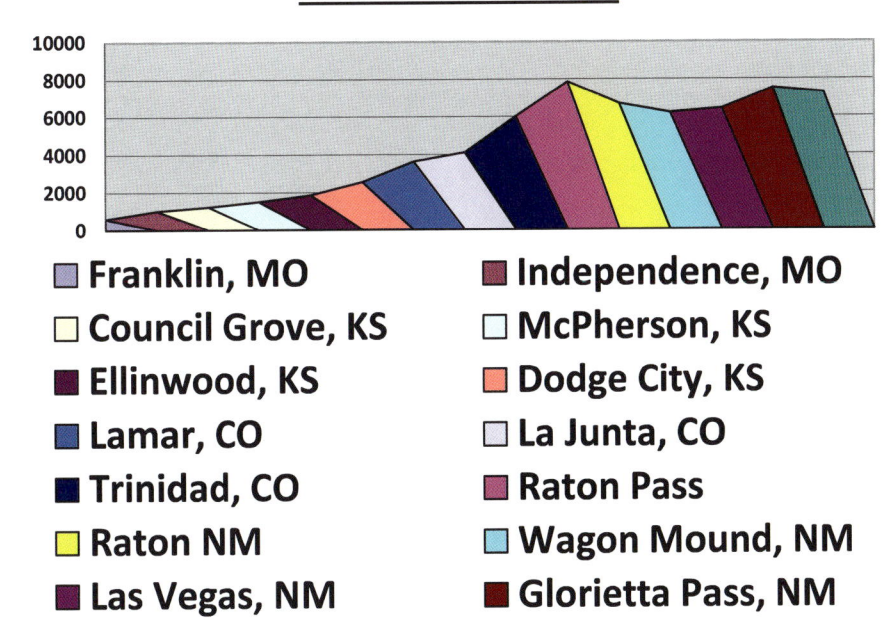

- Franklin, MO
- Council Grove, KS
- Ellinwood, KS
- Lamar, CO
- Trinidad, CO
- Raton NM
- Las Vegas, NM
- Santa Fe, NM
- Independence, MO
- McPherson, KS
- Dodge City, KS
- La Junta, CO
- Raton Pass
- Wagon Mound, NM
- Glorietta Pass, NM

Old Time Recipies

Recipe courtesy of 'Authentic INDIAN – MEXICAN Recipes', by William Hardwick, available at many of the gift shops along the Trail.

Carne De Olla

Originally, the ingredients were placed in an olla, a tempered pottery vessel used for carrying water, and placed close to the fire. It was prepared early in the day and was ready for the meal at sunset.

3 lbs cubed stew meat (any kind)
3 qts water
3 cups green beans (cut in 1 inch pieces)
12 2" pieces fresh corn on cob
6 yellow squash
8 squash blossoms (dried)
12 fresh green onions, cut in 1" pieces
1 section garlic clove
1 Tbsp coriander seeds, crushed
4 tsp salt.

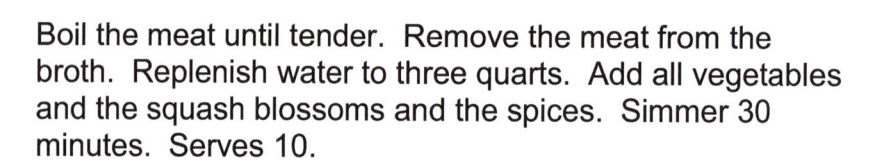

Boil the meat until tender. Remove the meat from the broth. Replenish water to three quarts. Add all vegetables and the squash blossoms and the spices. Simmer 30 minutes. Serves 10.

Mary's Cooking Tip:
Buy a 3 pound roast instead of packaged stew meat. Place the whole roast in a large Crockpot, and cook on low for 8 hours. Remove the meat from Crockpot and let it cool, then slip the meat out from the fat and gristle, and cut into bite size pieces.

Continue recipe in a large soup pot. Add enough water to broth from Crockpot to be 3 quarts, and go from there.

Recipe courtesy of 'Authentic INDIAN – MEXICAN Recipes', by William Hardwick, available at many of the gift shops along the Trail.

Chili Con Carne (Colorado) (Red)

This is an old, old recipe.

The best chili con carne is made with boiled beef. You may use any leftover meats and get excellent results. Trim all fat from the meat.

2 lbs boiling beef
2 Tbsp red chilli pwd
1 cup beef broth
1 cup tomatoes
1 large onion, finely chopped
6 coriander seeds

¼ tsp garlic pwd
1 tsp salt
1 tsp oregano
1 tsp cominos (cumin)
Cooking oil

Boil the meat, and when done cut into cubes no larger than ½ inch.

Sauté the onions until they are soft. In the hot oil, brown the boiled beef. Add all other ingredients and simmer 30 minutes with the pan covered. Remove any fats prior to serving.

Chili Verde Con Carne (Green)

Substitute 1 ½ cups of canned cooked green chilli for the 2 Tbsp red chilli powder in the above recipe

Mary's Cooking Tip: Cominos is an old name for Cumin. This recipe works well converted to a Crockpot instead of boiling the meat.

Recipe courtesy of '<u>Authentic INDIAN – MEXICAN Recipes</u>', by William Hardwick, available at many of the gift shops along the Trail.

Jalapeno Cornbread

2 ½ cups cornmeal
1 cup flour
1 onion well diced
1 tsp garlic salt
2 tsp sugar
1 cup creamed corn
1 cup grated Jack cheese

¼ cup cooking oil
2 eggs
1 tsp red chilli pwd
1 small can pimento
¼ cup milk – if needed
2 Tbsp baking pwd
6-12 canned Jalapenos, chopped fine

Drain all canned vegetables. Combine ingredients and mix well. Pour into a greased baking dish to a depth of one inch. Bake 45 minutes at 350 degrees. Serves 10.

<u>Mary's Cooking Tip</u>:
Delicious, hearty cornbread.; cooked up nicely in a large cast iron skillet. Mix the wet ingredients first, then add the dry ingredients.

Montage of Terrain Changes

From Eastern Kansas to the New Mexican High Plains

Gardner, KS vicinity, on Highway 56, not far from the big city of Kansas City, MO. Terrain on the Kansas prairie is green fields and blue skies for as far as you can see.

Tall Grass Prairie Historic Ranch area, south of Council Grove, KS, on Route 177 in Eastern Kansas. It appears flat when seen from a distance, but the terrain is actually consists of undulating hills and vales. Vernal pools appear in the low spots like in this photo.

On Highway US 56 in the vicinity of Ralph's Ruts in Kansas. It's a gravel road at this point. Green fields and blue skies for as far as you can see. It's like this for miles.

On Highway US 350, after leaving La Junta, CO. and turning south across the Purgatory River valley. The elevation is noticeably higher, and the air feels dry. It's colder, too.

Beautiful mesa formation seen from Highway US 350. We're not in Kansas anymore! The soil is much more sandy and dry.

Highway 350, traveling south towards Trinidad, CO. Cattle are resting in this high desert pasture, while in the background the Rocky Mountains are starting to appear.

Local Trinidad, CO, landmark, **Simpson's Rest**, elevation 6,462 feet.

The **Sangre de Cristo Mountains** (14,000), seen from Highway 25, are the southernmost of the mountain ranges that comprise the Rocky Mountains.

The name, Spanish for "blood of Christ", is said to come from the red color of the range at some sunrises and sunsets, especially when the mountains are covered with snow

Spanish Peaks - A pair of prominent volcanic mountains located in southwestern Colorado. The Ute Indians named them Huajatolla (pronounced Wa-ha-toy-a), meaning "two breasts". The Ute name translates as "Breasts of the Earth". The two peaks, West Spanish Peak (13,626 feet, on the left) and East Spanish Peak (12,683 feet, on the right) are part of the Sangre de Cristo range.

An important landmark on the Santa Fe Trail, the mountains can be seen as far north as Colorado Springs (133 miles), as far west as Alamosa (85 miles), points south to Raton, NM (65 miles), and points east of Trinidad, CO (up to 15 miles).

Turkey Mountains (7,877) off Highway US 25 have many different colored bands of rock.

Interstate 25 heading south after going thru Raton Pass. We are now on the high desert of New Mexico and heading straight for **Laughlin Peak** (7,761'). It's one of the dormant volcanoes that dot the high plains.

Interstate 25 – **Wagon Mound** is one of the most distinctive land formations on the Santa Fe Trail, is near our destination of Santa Fe.

The Rocky Mountains are made up of many individual mountain ranges, as shown here.

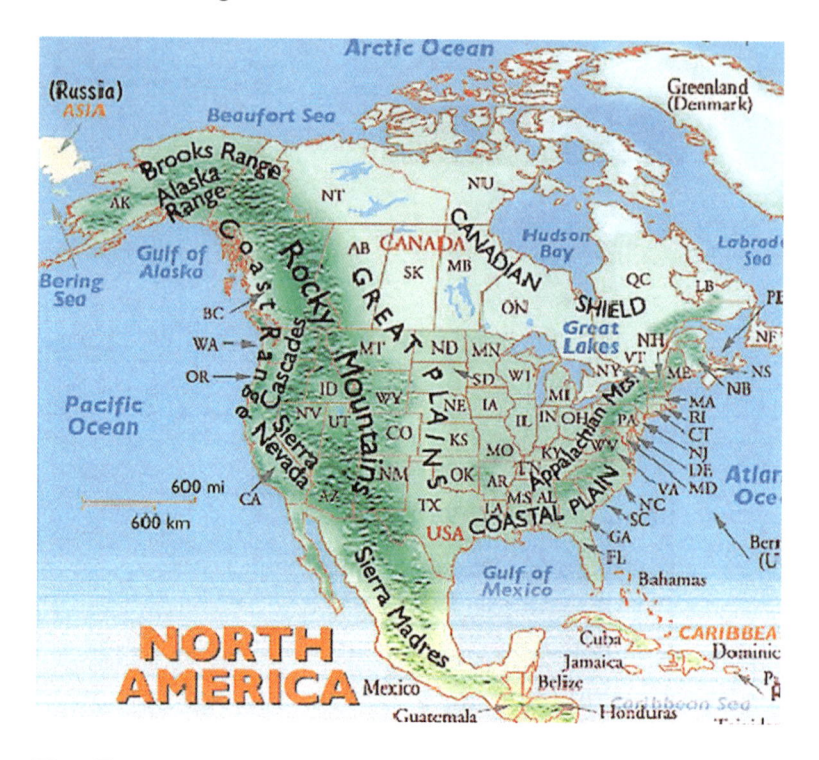

The Rocky Mountains are a major mountain system of western North America extending more than 3,000 miles from northwest Alaska to the Mexican border. The system includes numerous ranges and forms the Continental Divide. Its highest elevation is Mount Elbert, (14,433 ft), in central Colorado. In Canada the Rockies rise to 12,972 ft) at Mount Robson in eastern British Columbia. Sections of the mountains were explored by Coronado, Lewis and Clark, Zebulon Pike, Sir Alexander Mackenzie, and Simon Fraser.

http://en.wikipedia.org/wiki/Geography_of_the_United_States_Rocky_Mountain_System

References

Trail Dust
 A Quick Picture History of The Santa Fe Trail
By Gene and Mary Martin
Little London Press, 1972

Santa Fe Trail Trivia
By Leo E. Oliva and Bonita M. Oliva
Western Books, 1989

The Story of the Santa Fe Trail
By George W. Coffin, 1983,

I N D E X

A.R. Mitchell Museum 119
Albuquerque, NM 10
Arkansas River 8, 12, 15, 17, 79, 85, 93, 104
Baca House 120
Back N Thyme 24
Baird, James 11
barn 42, 45, 46
Becknell, William 11
Bent County Courthouse 94
Bent's Fort 18, 95, 101, 104
Big Timbers 92, 93
Bingham-Waggoner Estate .. 20
Bloom Mansion 120
Bonner Springs KS 24
Capulin Volcano National Monument 126
Chisholm Trail 52
Cimarron Crossing Bed & Breakfast 81
Cimarron Cutoff 77, 91, 130
Cimarron Cuttoff 69
Cimarron, KS 81
Clinton's Soda Fountain 16
Conestoga wagon 19, 88
Coronado 17, 58
Coronado Quivira 54
Cottage House 31
Council Oak 37, 38
Dodge City, KS 76, 77
dry route 69, 77
Edgerton, KS 29
Ellinwood, KS 56
Farmers & Drovers Bank 30
Father Hidalgo 11
Father Padilla 58
First National Bank 115
Fisher's Peak . 4, 111, 112, 118
Fort Larned 67, 68, 74
Fort Union 130, 131, 134
Franklin, MO 11
Fremont, John C. 101

Gardner, KS 27, 29, 149
Garfield, KS 76
Gift Shop Alert .. 20, 32, 43, 68, 95, 114, 126, 131
Gilbert, Whitney & Co 15
Glorietta Pass 136
Goat Hill 125
Harry S. Truman Library and Museum 23
Hays House Tavern and Restaurant 32
Hays, Seth M. 32
Independence, MO . 13, 18, 23, 136
Jackson County Courthouse 13
jail 36, 56, 72, 74
John Henry Restaurant 56
Jones, Stephan F 43
Just Taffy 14
Katy Depot 35
Kearney County Museum 87
Kinsley, KS 12, 76
La Fonda Hotel . 140, 142, 143, 144
La Junta, CO 12, 79, 95, 102
Lakin Train Station 90
Lamar, CO 33, 92
landmark 62, 64, 111, 112, 129, 141, 151, 152
Lanesfield School House 29
Last Chance Store 40
Laughlin Peak 122, 128
Loretto Chapel 143
Lyons, KS 54
Madonna of the Trail 30, 33, 34, 92
Mahaffie Stagecoach Stop and Farm 26
mail . 55, 59, 69, 77, 83, 84, 89, 108
Missouri Mules 28
M-K-T depot 35

156

Mountain Branch 69, 77, 83, 91, 110, 130
National Trails Museum. 18, 20
Neosho River 36, 39
Olathe, KS 12, 26
Palace of the Governors ... 137, 138
Pasaron Por Aqui 107
Pawnee Rock 62, 65, 66
Pawnee Rock, KS................ 63
Pike, Lt. Zebulon M.............. 11
Pinon Canyon Maneuver Site 108
post office 40
Raton Pass ... 12, 79, 112, 122, 123
Raton, NM 124
Recipe 146, 147, 148
Rheinland Restaurant.......... 14
Rocky Mountains 104, 136, 151, 152, 154
ruts...... 20, 60, 84, 85, 86, 106, 107, 135
Sangre de Cristo....... 110, 121, 128, 152

Santa Fe Plaza...............6, 137
Santa Fe Trail Center...........75
Santa Fe Trail Marker .59, 106, 135
Santa Fe Trail Museum......120
Santa Fe, NM 12, 137
Scaff Brothers.....................104
Sena Plaza 138
Sierra Grande.....................122
Simpson's Rest 113, 151
Spanish Peaks .. 110, 121, 152
Spring Hill Farm..............43, 46
Tarabino Inn 116
Terwilliger Home 41
The Station 38
Trinidad Trolley...................112
Trinidad, CO 12, 112, 114, 125
Truman, Harry S..............16, 23
Turkey Mountains.......128, 153
underground 56
Uptown Boutique 14
Wagon Mound.............129, 153
Watrous, NM 130
Wayside Chapel 76
wet route.........................69, 77

157

Made in the USA
Charleston, SC
05 January 2013